THE PRIVATE EYE ANNUAL 2005

EDITED BY IAN HISLOP

"Stop whinging. Everyone pees in the pool, don't they?"

Published in Great Britain by
Private Eye Productions Ltd
6 Carlisle Street, London W1D 5BN

© 2005 Pressdram Ltd
ISBN 1 901784 38 X
Designed by Bridget Tisdall
Printed and bound by
Butler and Tanner Ltd, Frome and London
2 4 6 8 10 9 7 5 3 1

THE PRIVATE EYE ANNUAL 2005

EDITED BY IAN HISLOP

"We aren't playing mummies and daddies –
*we **are** a mummy and daddy!"*

A YEAR IN PICTURES – 1

HEALTH SCARE

LEADERSHIP CHALLENGE

COMPASSION FATIGUE

SMACKING BAN

OLD JOKES REVISITED No. 94

BEDTIME STORY

THE GOLDFISH BOWL

EXCLUSIVE extracts from Cherie Blair's sensational behind-the-scenes bestseller about life in Number Ten Downing Street. Only in the Daily Cheriegraph!

Chapter One
Mrs Pitt The Younger

PITT THE Younger was a young dynamic politician who launched a courageous war against the tyrant Napoleon whom he believed was a threat to world peace and who possessed weapons of mass destruction (canon).

However, Pitt would never have been any good without the lifelong support of his wife Lady Cherina Pitt, the daughter of a poor, travelling player who, through her own abilities, rose to become the most powerful woman of her generation. She was also the first to install a water-closet in the upstairs bedroom of Number Ten Downing Street, which is still used today.

Chapter Two
Mrs Disraeli (*otherwise known as Queen Victoria*).

WITH HIS flamboyant waist-coats and exuberant oratory, 'Dizzy' Disraeli, as he was known, was most famous for being married to his wife Princess Cheriana, without whom he would not have been any good. Cheriana was also a celebrated cook who put the first Aga into the Number Ten kitchen.

Chapter Three
Lady Cheruntine Churchill

WINSTON CHURCHILL is known as the second greatest war leader in British History. Alone of the entire nation, he foresaw the threat of an evil dictator with a moustache. However, even he would not have been any good without his colourful consort, the beautiful and intelligent Lady Cheruntine, who stood by him through all his triumphs and tried to persuade him to give up smoking cigars in the bath (which she was the first to have installed).

Chapter Four
Mrs Cheryl Heath

Edward Heath was thought by many to have been a bachelor, but in fact our research has shown that he would never have been any good, had it not been for his secret wife and lifelong companion Mrs Cheryl Heath, the daughter of a Broadstairs Punch and Judy man.

It was she who introduced him to music and sailing and urged him to take Britain into the Common Market. She installed the first cinema organ in the Number Ten lounge.

Chapter Five
Mrs Norman Major

John Major would never have been (*That's enough wives. Ed.*)

© 2004, Mrs Cherie Booth and Lady Melvyna Barg.

HAPPY BIRTHDAY CHERIE

"Don't make a speech – we can't afford you"

THE SHAME OF LORD AND LADY BLACK

by Phil Boots

THE DISGRACEFUL behaviour of the former proprietor of the Daily Telegraph and his wife, Barbara Amielticket, has shocked the entire newspaper industry.

The spectacle of a proprietor fiddling his expenses, rather than a journalist, has appalled every member of the fourth estate.

This display of naked greed has, however, raised important questions for every self-respecting journalist. How come we didn't line our pockets instead of them? We should all hang our heads in shame and resign immediately.
© *Phil Boots 2004.*

MEMO TO EDITOR

Expenses incurred by Phil Boots in connection with writing above piece:

● 1st Class air ticket to New York for research purposes **£15,982**

● Set of Louis Vuitton luggage for above trip **£11,374**

● Jogging suit for chasing story **$250**

● Purchase of Rolls Royce to transport story to newsroom **£137,000**

● Party to celebrate 50th word written about Lady Black **£13,489**

● Copy of Lord Black's book on President Roosevelt from remainder shop **96p**

A selection of amazing statistics from Graydon Carter's new book 'Why I hate Bush like everyone else' (No. 578 on the Amazon "Best Book About George Bush Published This Week" list).

CARTER IN NUMBERS

12 Number of inches that should be cut off Graydon's silly hair.

56 Size of Graydon Carter's waist (in inches) after lunch.

1m Size of Graydon Carter's salary in dollars at 'Suits You' magazine, New York.

8 Number of wives married to Graydon Carter (so far).

7m number of boring articles about Hollywood stars printed in 'Suits You' this month.

1 Number of books by Graydon Carter sold this week. (Purchased with an I.O.U. by Mr C. Silvester)

94 Number of sycophantic pieces about Graydon Carter appearing this week by hacks who want a job on 'Suits You'.

What Ho McCrummy!

by the late P.G. Wodehouse

AN AIR of post-prandial somnolence had settled over the smoking room of the Drones Club.

The only sound that could be heard was the faint snoring of the Hon Bertram Wooster, as he sat in a deep armchair with a copy of *P.G. Wodehouse* by Robert McCrum draped over his face.

The book fell to the floor with a clatter, prompting a fellow Drone, "Gussie" Fink-Nottle, to comment "I say, Bertie, what's that tome you're swotting up on? Looks deadly dull. Certainly seems to have knocked you out for the count."

Bertie struggled out of the embraces of Morpheus to defend his fellow Drone, "Crummy" McCrum, who had laboured long and hard to produce his master-piece at the expense of several innocent Swedish forests.

"No, Gussie, it's jolly interesting. It's all about some writer johnny, who not only wrote loads of books but followed his old school's cricket scores in the paper even when he was 85."

"Gussie" was unimpressed.

"Wodehouse, eh? Didn't he get mixed up with that German bean with the moustache?"

Bertie looked worried. "I haven't got to that bit yet. I'm only up to page 1. But I can tell you, it's pretty gripping stuff."

"Gussie" looked as convinced as a penguin

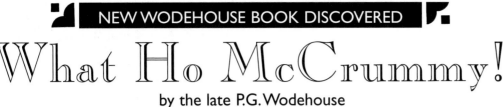

who has been approached by an enterprising refrigerator salesman in the middle of the Antarctic wastes.

"Look, it must be good!" protested Bertie. "The bally *Observer*, no less, calls it tophole stuff, and gives it a massive spread."

AT THAT moment the head of "Barmy" Fotheringay-Phipps loomed up over his copy of the *Sporting Life*.

"Don't be such a chump, Bertie," he scoffed. "Friend McCrummy is the *Observer*'s books editor. That's why he plastered it all over his own pages calling it the book of the century."

"But what about the other papers then?" persisted Bertie. "Their book chaps all crack it up as well."

"That's because they're all chums of McCrummy's!" explained an exasperated "Barmy".

"I say, that's dashed clever of him," gasped the astounded Wooster, deeply impressed. "He must eat a lot of fish."

Cast In Full

Crummy McCrum	HUGH LAURIE
Bertie Woofter	STEPHEN FRY
Lord Ha Ha	P.G. WODEHOUSE

Continuing The Sensational Serialisation Of The

Andrew Marr Story

CHAPTER 94

Why no one read the Independent when I was editor

WHEN I met the Deputy Night Features Chief on that Friday by the water-cooler in the open-plan office at Canary Wharf to discuss the redesign of the local government pages and the positioning of the cross-word, it was clear for some reason that nobody was reading the z-z-z-z-z

© *Andrew No-marr-please.*

GLENDA SLAGG

■ JOHN MORTIMER!?! Now I've heard it all!?!? Randy old Rumpole had Britian's favourite Mum up the duff forty years ago!?!? What a disgrace!?

Oi, Rumpy-Pumpole — couldn't you keep your briefs on (Geddit?!?!) for five minutes?!?! And what about the poor little nipper who for all those years never knew his dear old dad who was guzzling champagne with his showbiz pals down at the Ivy!?! Justice?! Don't make me laugh!! My verdict on you, Sir John Nortiboy (Geddit?!) is that you should be strung up!?!?

■ THREE CHEERS for Sir John!?! What a heartwarming story for dear old Rumpole, in the autumn of his days, to find out he's a dad at 97!?!? And who's the lucky gal?! Wonderful Wendy Craig — the nation's number-one Mum?!? 'Scuse me, Mister, I'm just goin' to shed a tear!?!?

Byeeee!!!

7

What's Wrong With Falling Leaves?

Asks The World's Worst Columnist **Max Hastings**

WHAT a silly fuss some people make at this time of year over leaves falling off trees.

They complain that our streets are clogged up, that our entire train network grinds to a halt, and that even the Diana Memorial Fountain ceases to operate because of excess leaves.

Talk about moaning minnies! Falling leaves are as much a part of our British way of life as buttered toast, chicken tikka masala and the Queen Mother!

I for one am not ashamed to stand up and be counted when it comes to the Great Leaves Debate!

There's nothing finer, in my humble opinion, than the crunch of freshly fallen leaves under one's Wellingtons, as one heads off with one's dog for a day's shooting or fishing.

What would the politically correct health-and-safety-mad brigade suggest that we should do with all the leaves that nature has so bountifully showered upon us?

Sweep them up in a pooper-scooper and send them off to the Third World for starving peasants to turn them into sandals? Whose daft idea was that? (*Yours. Ed.*)

No. I say leave our leaves alone. They never did harm to anyone, and they are a damn sight better than covering the whole country in concrete, which is what Mr Prescott would prefer us to walk on.

© Hastingstrash Columnar Services

NEXT WEEK: Max Hastings on "What have people got against breakfast?"

That All-Purpose Football Editorial In Full

ENGLAND's pathetic/inspired performance last night has left manager Sven-Goran Eriksson/Sven-Moron Gonowson with only one option – resign, you bastard/please accept a knighthood. Your decision to give the hardworking and loyal/fat and lazy David Beckham the captaincy has turned out to be a complete disaster/tactical masterstroke.

And now it is perfectly clear that the proud England team/bunch of losers will go all the way to win the World Cup/will not even qualify for the World Cup.

So we say, '*Sod/Hats off to Sven*'!

TORY RESHUFFLE

I want new blood

GLOBAL CRISIS

At last the government is taking action on the issues that really matter

---

"We need to raise your profile, Miss Austen. Have you considered celebrity wrestling?"

Haldane.

JOIN THE ARMY

Have You Got What It Takes?

● **Could you survive sexual abuse during training?**

● *Could you avoid committing suicide?*

● **Could you then go to Iraq and be charged with murder if you haven't already been shot by the Americans?**

● *Could you face a lifetime in jail?*

If you think you've got what it takes to join the Modern Army then you are what we are looking for.

Your Country Needs You!

BLAIR OUTRAGED AT COMMONS INVASION

by Our Political Staff **John Sergeant-at-Arms**

THE PRIME Minister yesterday expressed his fury at the invasion of the House of Commons. He told reporters, "The House of Commons is no place for people expressing opinions about Government policy.

The House of Commons is meant to be empty so that my policies go through unopposed.

"How dare these hooligans come into the chamber and try and debate the issues? It is an affront to autocracy." *(Surely "Democracy"? Ed.)*

THE DAILY TELEGRAPH   Friday, October 1, 2004

Letters *to the Editor*
Liberty under threat

SIR – As one of many millions of patriotic pro-hunt protestors who travelled to London to exercise their democratic right to stage a peaceful demonstration in Parliament Square, I would like to put it on record that our once-admired British police force behaved with all the savagery of Nazi stormtroopers in some third-world banana republic, which is surely what we are heading for under the despotic dictatorship of the Fascist Blair and his grinning wife Evita, who personally ordered their Stasi-trained riot police to hit me over the head with their truncheons when my only "offence" was to have asked one of them "Excuse me, officer, is this the way to Parliament Square?".
Norman Voletrouser
The Old Cottage Hospital,
Bigglesworth, Beds

SIR – I wish to salute the six brave and high-spirited young chaps who had the nerve and the wit to invade the House of Commons in order to exercise their democratic right to protest against the most iniquitous piece of legislation that has been forced on the British people. These heroic young men, reminiscent of the 20-year-olds who saved Britain in the summer of 1940, offered no threat to anyone, and when asked to leave, did so without any fuss and with the same good manners that they showed on entering the chamber. I say "Hats off" to these gallant champions of democracy.
Lucinda Topes
The Old Ferry,
Ringworm,
Hants

The Guardian   Friday October 1 2004

Letters

Democracy at risk

As one of the many millions of ordinary television viewers who oppose hunting, can I record my pleasure and delight in seeing the bloodied faces of the elderly and privileged toffs who the police quite rightly beat over the head for trying to thwart the democratically expressed will of the people by opposing the totally justified ban on hunting with dogs. Now these arrogant Tories know how the miners felt when they were gunned down by Thatcher's armed militia during the poll tax riots at Wapping, not to mention how the fox feels when it is torn apart limb from limb by braying members of the landed gentry and other friends of the Royal family. At last Blair has done something decent, to atone for his war crimes (on the subject of which I have written to you on a number of previous occasions).
Steve Beard
The Old Squat, Hackney

● The outrageous and sickening breach of security by six public school-educated hoorays in breaking into the Mother of Parliaments shows how vital it is to have a complete overhaul of the antiquated so-called "security system" operated by men in tights, many of whom also went to public schools. What would have happened if these intruders had been fully paid-up suicide bombers from Al Qaeda exercising their democratic right to protest against the war in Iraq, er, to my mind these irresponsible toff anarchists should have been shot on sight. Then they'd know how the fox feels when it is being torn apart limb from limb by the Duke of Edinburgh.
Dave Rollup
The New Squat, Islington

Who are they – the countryside six who brought democracy to its knees?

Jeremy Ravenscroft-Starborgling, 18, a close friend of Prince Harry's. Educated at St Cakes, the famous Midlands public school. Jeremy's father is Master of the Dumpster Hunt in Devon.

Rupert Starborgling-Ravenscroft, 19, a close friend of Prince William's, who plays polo for the Old Cakeians. His father, Sir Hugo Greenwelly, is Master of the Massingberd Foxhounds in Leicestershire.

Kevin Prole, 21, not a close friend of any member of the Royal Family. Educated at the Chuter Ede Comprehensive in Slough, Prole runs a fashionable Chelsea bistro, "Les Deux Sausages Avec Frites". *(That's enough toffs, Ed.)*

BRIAN CLOUGH DIES
Tributes pour in

by Our Football Staff **E.I.Adieu**

Are we there yet?

MAYFLOWER

PLYMOUTH

THE WORLD of football was rocked to its foundations last night by the tragic passing of a man they called simply "Brian Clough".

As tributes poured in from all over the world (but mainly Derby), leading former manager, Brian Clough, summed up the feelings of the entire football fraternity.

"Cloughie," he said, "was simply the greatest football manager of all time. There was no one to touch me, and there never will be."

His thoughts were echoed by the legendary Brian Clough, who said, "Just look at my record. All the rest of the managers in history are rubbish. I am and always will be the best."

But perhaps the most touching tribute of all came from the man who knew him best, Brian Clough.

"Brian" he said, "knew more about football management than all the rest put together. If there was a Nobel prize for football, I would have a cupboard full of them."

Clough tributes in full: p. 94-160

2004
by George Orwell

IT was a bright, cold day in April, and the clocks were striking thirteen. Winston Smith, his chin nuzzled into his breast in an effort to escape the vile wind, slipped quickly through the glass doors of Victory Mansions, though not quickly enough to prevent a swirl of gritty dust from entering along with him.

As he entered the Ministry of Truth building, the words of the great leader continued to echo in Winston's ears... *"The war with Iraq is over, The war with Iraq has just begun"* (cont. p. 94)

POLLY FILLER

HOW dare Patricia Hewitt tell us all we've got to have more babies? The women of this country are *already* looking after enough babies, ie their useless menfolk!

Who needs another selfish, incompetent dependent when you've already got one called Simon sitting slumped in front of "Grumpy Old Men" starring A.A. Gill and Rick Wakeman, nodding his head as though any of them told us something we didn't know, like, for instance, how useless men are?

I'LL tell you what annoys *me* about modern life – it's people who don't empty the dishwasher and don't turn up to Charlie's parents' evening at St Tweedles School for Dispraxic Over-Achievers because there's a repeat of Jeremy Clarkson's Extreme Tank Racing from Qatar on the Testosterone Channel! That's what gets *my* goat!

So don't talk to me about babies, Ms Hewitt. What you're proposing is the Nanny State – and Polly Filler for one is having none of it.

Nannies are too expensive, especially when you can get an au pair from Haiti for less than £1 an hour!! And Delphine *does* know where the dishwasher is and is grateful that it's not blowing around the house!!

Who loves ya, baby? Not Polly Filler!

© Polly Filler in all newspapers.

WORLD'S MOST EXPENSIVE BOOK PUBLISHED
No Copies Sold

by Our Literary Staff
Professor Rowan Pelling, Chair of Erotic Studies at the University of Filth *(formerly the Raymond Revuebar Polytechnic)*

THE WORLD's longest-ever book has been published today, costing £4 million. The new 'Dictionary of Everyone Who's Ever Lived' contains 2 billion entries, has taken 25 years to compile and contains more words than there are grains of sand in the Sahara.

All Must-Have Entries

For the first time, the Oxford DEWEL (formerly the DNB) includes the names of the entire dead population of the British Isles, up to the year 2000.

Professor Brian Greyman, who masterminded the biggest single project since the Pyramids, said last night, "our new all-inclusive policy means that, for the first time, women, the disabled and members of the ethnic communities are at last properly represented, not to mention all those obscure, ordinary people who may not have done anything worth remembering but who have a perfect right not to be excluded from such a vital research tool".

Here are just some of the millions of new entries whose details have been included in the greatest book ever published.

Ethelreda the Unwilling *(806?-817?)* Ethelreda was the second daughter of Ethelred the Ever Ready and his wife Ribena. Nothing is known of her life or indeed that of her parents, but it has been suggested that she may have lived near the East Anglian settlement of Hutton Hoo.

Warren Onanugu *(1962-1999)* Earned his place in history as the Nigerian-born, Paddington-based wineshop manager who once sold a plastic bag of clinking bottles to a Conservative Chancellor of the Exchequer, the Rt. Hon. Norman Lamont.

Captain James Hook *(apocryphal)* Possibly the best-known disabled Old Etonian of his generation. Served as self-appointed Governor of the Neverneverland Islands, and was notorious for the brutality with which he suppressed the so-called "Lost Boys Revolt", led by the charismatic human rights campaigner Wendy Darling and her male assistant Peter Pan.

The longest entry in the book is for the late Diana, Princess of Wales, taking up an entire volume.

"We are particularly proud of this entry," said Professor Greyman, "because it might get us some publicity, and she is the only person that the public has ever heard of."

The 'Dictionary of Everyone Who's Ever Lived' is available at www.mostexpensivebookintheworld.com for only £7,500 a month.

WHO ELSE IS IN

Fanny Hill
White Van Man
Monty Python
Cyril the Squirrel
(cont. p. 9,999,994)

GLENDA SLAGG
THE BRIGHTON BELLE! (GEDDIT?)

■ SHED A TEAR for poor Billie 'n' Chris!?!? That's Evans and Piper, stoopid!?!? We thought their marriage would last forever! He – successful middle-aged TV millionaire. She – the 17-year-old pop sensation. Who would have thought that their love would wither and die after their flame had burned so brightly for so long?!?

I would have been more surprised if the Rock of Gibraltar had melted into the sea, apes and all, rather than read that Billie 'n' Chris would not walk arm in arm down Lovers' Lane into old age for ever – and so much in love?!?! Gulp!?!?

■ BILLIE AND CHRIS!?!? I told you it wouldn't last!?!? The marriage of this pissed-up Grandad and his child bride was as likely to last as the Rock of Gibraltar is to melt into the sea, apes and all?!?! If ever there was a mismatch, this was it!?!? He – the washed-up DJ with a drink problem and money to burn. She – the star-crazed teenage golddigger. They were hardly going to walk arm in arm down Lovers' Lane into old age for ever, were they? And, as for love – pull the other one, Mister!?!?!?!

■ HATS OFF to Britney Spears and the lucky geezer she's just got hitched to?!?!? Now there's a marriage that's going to last for ever!?!?! Trust me, they are so much in love that

Madam Glenda is looking into her crystal ball and ordering champagne to toast their silver wedding anniversary!??!?

■ HAPPY BIRTHDAY to Sophia Loren, the dark-eyed diva who's more sexy at seventy than all the others put together!?!? This sultry sex siren of the silver screen proves that us mature gals can still have the fellas a-groanin' and a-moanin', a-dribblin' and a-wibblin', a-peerin' and a-leerin' *(That's enough. Ed.)*

Saluté Senora Loren! You are an inspirazzione to all us Senoritas who are looking at the wrong side of 69!?!?! Geddit!!?!

Buenas noches, Sophia, on your big day!?!?

■ HERE THEY ARE – Glenda's 'Fall' Guys!?! Geddit?!?!

● **Alan Titchmarsh** – There's an Area of Natural Beauty you might want to explore with your green fingers!?!? *(You're fired. Ed.)*

● **Rolf Harris** – I'll be your Mona Lisa, Rolfie, but make sure you bring your didgeridoo to give me that certain smile!?!?! *(You're still fired. Ed.)*

● **Cat Stevens** – Don't worry, Beardy – I'll let you in anytime!?!?!? *(Clear your desk immediately. Ed.)*

Byeeee!!!

GOVERNMENT DEMANDS BABIES

We need more people born yesterday

"...and here's one of us 20 seconds ago"

The Daily Torygraph

THE PAPER THAT SUPPORTS OUR BORIS

Friday, October 1, 2004

We'll fight on, our cause is just – we shall never give in to the terrorists...

...and now back to the Northern Ireland talks

HUNTER

Pathetic Lib Dems Top Poll

BY OUR POLITICAL STAFF FRANK JOHNSON AND DANIEL JOHNSON

NO-HOPER Charles Kennedy is all set to lead his bunch of losers to their best ever election result, according to a poll commissioned by this paper from notyou.gov.

The drunken and universally-derided Lib Dem leader scores the highest personal popularity rating of all the party leaders, gaining a dismal 86 percent approval, compared to Michael Howard's fast-rising 2 percent figure.

When voters were asked, "Which party do you trust most on the issue of pensions?", it was the sandal-wearing, cardigan-eating, vegetarian, lesbian non-smokers who came out on top, with a miserable 94 percent.

All this adds up to a week of woe for 'Chat-show Charlie', as the Lib Dems are so demoralised that they cannot even mount a proper leadership challenge.

A Taxi Driver writes

Every week a well-known cab driver is invited to comment on an issue of topical importance.

THIS WEEK: **'Greg' Dyke**, Cab No. 4650, on the current standing of the prime minister.

"I don't mind admitting, I used to have a lot of time for Tony. I even gave him some money once, 5,000 quid, which was a lot of money in those days. Course now, it's nuffink, no more than the fare from Hounslow to Shepherds Bush via Norwich. But that Blair, if you ask me, he's blown it. No one would believe a word he says about anything, would they? As for his mate Campbell, what a bastard! All them lies they told us about the war and everything. Bleedin' tosser, Blair, innee? I tell you what, I really hate him! You know what I'd do to him if I had my way? I'd string him up off that London Eye, going round and round with a noose round his neck! What a bastard? Where was it, you said you were going, guv? Sorry, we're going the other way. I had those BBC governors in the back of the cab once. What a load of wankers. Stuck up gits. Dame Pauline Neville-Jones! What's she ever done? Blimey. I think I'm going to have a cardiac arrest. I'll have to pull in to take my tablets. I'd take a bus if I were you, guv. I think I've had enough for one night.

© Sir Gregorian Dyke, former Director General of the British Broadcasting Corporation.

THE LIFE OF DR JONATHAN

By His Devoted Disciple James Boswell

I called upon my friend and mentor Dr Jonathan at his lodgings in Charlotte Street to learn of his new project, to wit, a Compendium of Disbelief, to be transmitted via Mr Logie Baird's televisual device. I found the good doctor surrounded by the great savants of our age, namely Professor Dawkins from the ancient University of Oxenforde and Dame Toynbee, the celebrated blue-stocking.

Boswell: Surely you are not disputing that there must be a benevolent superior being, one fully cogniscent with all human knowledge, who surveys the world from a position of omniscience, and who mere mortals cannot comprehend?

Dr Jonathan (*smiling*): Indeed, sir, 'tis myself.

(Ends)

GOVERNMENT ANNOUNCES NEW EDUCATION FUCK-UP

by Our Education Staff

THE GOVERNMENT today announced a radical fuck-up of the entire secondary education system aimed at reversing the decline in standards and the failure to produce employable school-leavers.

"It is high time for another fuck-up," said the author of the government's new report, Michael Tomlinson.

"We haven't fucked up schools since the big fuck-up when we introduced AS Levels and the fuck-ups before that when we introduced GCSEs, coursework, continuous assessment and all the other bright ideas that have made the education system what it is today."

Mr Tomlinson said: "This is the fuck-up to end all fuck-ups."

APOLOGY

We apologise to readers for the typographical errors in the above piece, where the word "shake" has been inadvertently replaced each time by the word "fuck". This may have led to a regrettable change in the overall interpretation by readers of the likely success of the radical reforms instituted by Mr Tomlinson and we regret any confusion caused.

OXFORD CLASS LIST
WORKING
MIDDLE

Nevin.

Was Prince Harry Given Help In His Art 'A' Level? *You Decide*

Harry's Final Coursework Project *(Grade B)*

What's Wrong With Flu?

Asks The World's Worst Columnist MAX HASTINGS

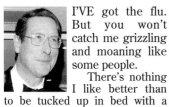

I'VE got the flu. But you won't catch me grizzling and moaning like some people.

There's nothing I like better than to be tucked up in bed with a temperature of 104 degrees, a hacking cough, a raging headache and feeling like death warmed up.

It's a wonderful autumn tradition. Which is why I say to all those whingers who complain that they've got the dreaded lurgy, "Rejoice. There's nothing to beat a healthy dose of good, old-fashioned, British flu."

© Hitlertrash Productions 2004.
Exclusive to all newspapers.

"Hey lads, Terry doesn't know any catchphrases from Little Britain!"

A Century Of New Words

A sensational new book **Howlers And Bummers** – the 'language report' – has provided Britain's editors with a wonderful excuse for filling up whole pages with lists of words, instead of having to think up any ideas.

The book, by top TV language expert, **Suzi Dunce**, of the *Countupyourmoney* programme, shows how many familiar buzz words in fact came into fashion long before you would imagine.

Here is Suzi's eye-opening list, which tells us how we lived and what we said in the hundred years of the 20th Century:

1904 Jet Lag

1905 Sellotape

1906 Kentucky Fried Chicken

1907 Weapons of Mass Destruction

1908 Hip Hop

1909 Google

And that's just the first decade. Some periods were particularly fertile for these new words which were soon on everybody's lips. Such a time was the Second World War:

1939 Walking Stick

1940 Mange-Tout

1941 Art Deco

1942 Hitler

1943 Fish Fingers

1944 Bling-Bling

1945 Good Evening

But even this period was nothing compared to the Sixties, perhaps the most prolific decade for buzz words of all time. Ms Dunce singles out, for instance:

1960 Flappers

1961 Maltesers

1962 iPod

1963 Spud-U-Like

1964 New Labour

The list carries on right up to the present day. The big vogue word this year, according to Ms Dunce, has been:

2004 Old Rope (what apparently a great many editors are prepared to give money for)

PIG DENIES 'SEXUAL RELATIONS' WITH REBECCA LOOS

by our Agricultural Staff
PHIL TEST-TUBE

A FURIOUS pig today strongly denied claims by celebrity slapper Rebecca Loos that she had "pleasured" him in a sty during an afternoon of passion.

"I am a happily married pig", he told reporters, "and I love my wife and piglets very much. I even have a tattoo of young Pinky on my back." He continued: "Do I look like the sort of pig who would have to get his thrills with the likes of Rebecca Loos?"

Pig in a Poke

But last night a spokesman for Rebecca Loos, Mr Max Clifford, said: "My client stands by her story. She and the pig had an intense relationship lasting several minutes and I've got the pictures to prove it."

David Beckham is 28.

THE Sun SAYS

HOW LOW can television stoop showing scenes of disgusting bestiality between a woman and a pig that have never before been screened in Britain.

If you haven't seen them turn to pages 2,3,4,5,6 and 7 to see exactly how revolting and depraved these amazing pictures really are!

PLUS

Your chance to win a posh night out with Britain's sexiest pig **p.8**

ME AND MY SPOON

THIS WEEK

CHERIE BLAIR

Are there any particular types of spoons that you and Tony prefer?

If you are referring to the Prime Minister, I have made it a firm rule that I am never, under any circumstances, prepared to talk about our private life together, and that applies as much to spoons as it does to anything else.

Your friend Carole Caplin has said that spoons can have healing properties when they are pointed in the direction of certain Inca holistic sites. Would you agree?

I've made it a firm rule that I am never, under any circumstances, prepared to talk about my private life, and that applies just as much to my relationship with Carole Caplin as it does to what spoons Tony uses to stir his coffee – which, incidentally, is decaffeinated these days and sugar-free, so he doesn't need a spoon anyway. Okay?

Mrs Blair, you said that you would only agree to do this interview if we turned it into a plug for your new book 'The Spoons of Downing Street'. Wasn't there an amusing story about Lady Dorothy Macmillan, President de Gaulle and a soup spoon that was by mistake left in the fridge?

I've no idea – I didn't write that bit.

When you move to Connaught Square, will you take your spoons with you, or will you be buying new ones?

That question is off-limits for the purposes of this interview.

Has anything amusing ever happened to you in connection with a spoon?

You will be hearing from my solicitors.

NEXT WEEK: *Jeremy Irons, 'Me And My Irons'*

I Remember, I Remember

I remember, I remember,
The house where I was born,
The little window where the sun
Came peeping in at morn;
He never came a wink too soon,
Nor brought too long a day,
But now, I often wish the night
Would have sodomised him up the
fucking arse.

If

If you can keep your head when all
about you
Are losing theirs to the American
fucking bastards
Who couldn't give a fucketty shit
whether
Your fucking head stays on your neck
or bloody not;
If you can talk with crowds and keep
your virtue
Or walk with Kings – and tell them to
shut the fuck up.
If neither foes nor loving friends can
hurt you
Because they've just blown the fucking
bollocks off you
Yours is the Earth and all the fucking
piss that's in it,
And – which is more – you can eat shit,
my son!

The Lake Isle of Innisfree

I will arise and go now, and go to
Innisfree
And a small cabin build there, of clay
and wattles made;
Nine bean-rows will I have there, a hive
for the honey-bee,
Until the Yanks come along and fuck the
shit out of it.

Home Thoughts from Abroad

Oh, to be in England
Now that April's there
And whoever wakes in England
Sees, some morning, unaware,
That stinky fucker Mr Tony fucking
Blair,
And says, Look, chum, get off my
fucking land
You're trespassing so wipe that fucking
smile
Off your fucking face and fuck the
fuck off.

Horatius

Lars Porsena of Clusium
By the Nine Gods he swore
That the great house of Tarquin
Shouldn't get its nose ground
In the shit any fucking more.

We'll Go No More A-Roving

We'll go no more a-roving
So late into the night,
Certainly not if the Blair fascists
Have their fucking way
And gag myself and Lady Antonia
And leave us head-first in a fucking
gutter
Somewhere South of Holland Park.

Daffodils

I wandered lonely as a cloud
That floats on high o'er vales and hills
When all at once I saw a crowd,
A host, of golden daffodils.
And I said, come on, Lady Antonia,
Get your coat on, I'm not standing
For any more of this fucking nonsense
Those fucking daffodils have got it in
for us
It's free speech they can't abide.

Elegy Written in a Country Churchyard

The curfew tolls the knell of parting day
The lowing herd wind slowly o'er the lea
And the ploughman homeward plods his
weary way
Until the bomb goes off, his head is
smashed to blazes
And his hand is blown to fucking
smithereens
And his ploughman's lunch ends up in a
fucking puddle, all wet and soggy.

The Charge of the Light Brigade

Half a league, half a league,
Half a league onward,
All in the valley of Death
Rode the six hundred.
On the direct orders of Mein Fuhrer
Blair:
Thanks a fucking bunch, chum.

O No John!

On yonder hill there stands a creature
So who the fuck are you, chum?

Cargoes

Quinquireme of Nineveh from distant
Ophir
Rowing home to haven in sunny
Palestine,
With a cargo of ivory,
And apes and peacocks,
Sandalwood, cedarwood, and sweet
white wine.
They blew them into fucking shit.
They are eating it.
Now I want you to come over here and
kiss me on the arse, chum.

The Owl and the Pussy Cat

The Owl and the Pussy-Cat went to sea
In a beautiful pea-green boat.
They took some honey, and plenty of
money
Because they were fucking Yanks
Sucking the shit out of the arse of the
poor.

Come into the Garden, Maud

Come into the garden, Maud,
For the black bat, Night, has flown:
Come into the garden, Maud,
For I am here at the gate alone,
Sniffing the pong of the dead.

The Tiger

Tiger! Tiger! burning bright
In the forests of the night,
The big pricks are out.
They'll fuck everything.
Watch your back.

As told to
CRAIG BROWN

Glenda Slagg Pays Tribute To The Living Legend Who Died Yesterday – Lynda Lee-Potter, the First Lady of Fleet Street

A whole nation is united in grief, as every man, woman and child in Britain mourns the death of the woman who spoke for Middle England.

And not just Middle – but the entire country, rich and poor, young and old, male and female.

She was fearless, bold and without fear.

She voiced what every single person was thinking, but did not have the courage, the ability or the talent to put into words.

And what words they were! By turns waspish, outspoken, witty, poignant, heart-rending, wry, spry, dry, gritty, grotty,

waspy, wispy... there are simply not enough words in the dictionary to begin to describe the towering yet petite figure who for 30 years has dominated British journalism like no one else.

LYNDA – THE TRIBUTES FLOW IN

Kofi Annan: I shall miss her pungent comments on world affairs more than I can say.

Saddam Hussein: She was firm but fair. I valued her opinions.

President George W. Bush: A very great writer who spoke

for Middle Earth.

Tony Blair: I agree with whatever the President says.

Big Brother's Nadia: She was warm, she was witty, she was wise. She was the Jane Austen of our time. Is that what you'd like me to say?

Exclusive to all newspapers

Paula Radcliffe
An Apology

IN COMMON with all other newspapers, we may have given the impression that we considered Ms Paula Radcliffe's career to be over and that furthermore her Olympic performances had in some way let the nation down. Headlines such as "Pathetic Paula Turns On The Tears", "Why Don't You Try The Disabled Marathon, You Hopeless Crybaby?" and "Drop Dead, You Loser!" may have led readers to infer that we considered Ms Radcliffe as a less than competent competitor in the field of long-distance running.

Following her victory in the New York Marathon, we now realise that Ms Radcliffe is an outstanding athlete who proudly represents her country at the highest level and should be given suitable recognition of her services to the nation in the form of a Damehood (see piece "Arise Dame Paula, Britain's Golden Girl and Marathon Marvel").

We would like to apologise unreservedly to our readers for any misunderstanding following earlier reports.

© All newspapers

Words That Will Live Forever

Here are just some of the immortal jewels which tripped so effortlessly from Lynda's tireless word processor:

On Princess Di

"*Aren'tchasickofher? Spoiled, pampered, publicity-crazed, mad, a life-size barbie doll, with anorexia thrown in.*" 29 Sept 1997

"*Beautiful, brave, compassionate and caring – I don't mind admitting that I wept buckets when I heard that Diana was cruelly taken from us. And anyone who remained dry-eyed should be strung up.*" 30 Sept 1997

On Food, Drink And Everything Else

"*...bottled water – what a waste of money! And it tastes disgusting. When we were kids we just had water out of the tap – and it tasted delicious. I wouldn't give that bottled rubbish to my cat.*" 12 July 1985

"*Kids today – they don't know how lucky they are! In the old days we were all dying of typhoid because of that evil-smelling tap water that our grandmothers made us drink. Now they can go to the local shop and buy a 2-litre bottle of that sparkling, pure, clear-as-a-mountain spring water for as little as £10.*" 13 July 1985

On Elaine Paige

"*What a talentless, useless cow – and rude too!*" 7 March 1992

"*What a talentless, useless cow that Elaine Paige is – and rude with it!*" 8 March 1992

"*Who gets my vote as the rudest, most useless, least talented cow in show business? You guessed it, mister – Elaine Paige.*" 9 March 1992

Gypsies To Take Over Your Daily Mail

by Our Panic Staff
Terry Fied and **Al Armist**

IT's the nightmare scenario – and there's no stopping it. Gypsies have moved into the Daily Mail and you can't get rid of them.

Every day they are taking more and more space and soon experts predict they will have settled on every page of the newspaper, forcing out decent, ordinary stories about immigrants and asylum seekers. Within weeks there will be nothing left in your paper but gypsies and the rubbish that comes with these *(cont. p. 94)*

On Other Pages ● How these gypsy stories will reduce the value of stories about falling house prices.

MIDDLE-OF-THE-ROAD RAGE

THE NIGHTMARE SCENARIO THAT JUSTIFIED THE INVASION OF IRAQ

by Jack Straw

SO, the truth is out. The weapons inspectors' latest report has at last revealed just how close the world came to Armageddon thanks to Saddam Hussein's weapons of mass destruction.

OK, he didn't have any. But the reality was much more frightening.

If Saddam had decided to develop these weapons, which he didn't, and had the money to do so, which he hadn't, then he could, within a matter of only 45 years, have initiated terrifying programmes of the type that didn't exist to produce devastating nuclear, chemical and biological megadeath missiles which, if they were launched on launchers of the type they didn't have, would have laid waste the entire planet, allowing Saddam to conquer the world and run it as an Islamic superstate in collaboration with hostile alien insect life forms who would land in the West to harvest all the remaining human beings to feed their dying planet Kreuxxl in the Zebulon sector of Andromeda Five... Excuse me, I think I had better go and lie down.

© *Jack Straw 2004.*

That Iraq Honours List In Full

(cont. from page one)

Order of the Whitewash
Lord Hutton, First Class
Lord Butler, Second Class

The Companion of Dishonour
Mr Alastair Campbell; Mr John Scarlett; Mr Geoffrey Hoon; Mr Jack Straw; Mr Jonathon Powell; The Conservative Party.

The Iraq Cross
Field Marshall Sir Anthony Blair VC, DSO, etc *(That's enough Gongs, Ed).*

RUMSFELD NEW LINK CLAIM

THE American Secretary of Defense Mr Donald Rumsfeld yesterday admitted that there was no link between himself and the truth.

"I have seen no evidence," he said, "to connect anything I say with the reality of what is actually happening."

He quoted as an example his claim that there was a link between Saddam Hussein and the terrorist organisation Al Qaeda.

"That claim was hogwash," he said. "I was lying. You can't trust anything I say."

He later retracted this statement, saying "When I said I was lying, I was in fact lying. As indeed I am now. I hope that makes it clear."

"I can't find that WMD report"

POLLY FILLER

IT'S the biggest challenge of modern motherhood – juggling modern motherhood with promoting your book about the challenge of modern motherhood!

Yes, *'More Mummy For Old Rope'* (Tyrell and Johnson £8.99) is in the shops now – a hilarious sideways look at negotiating the daily tightrope of school runs, children's parties, dead hamsters, useless partners and linguistically challenged au-pairs!!

And now it's hot off the presses, how on earth am I meant to combine doing an interview on Radio Shropshire's 'Night Cap' (the late-night phone-in for night owls in the Shropshire area) with dealing with toddler Charlie's homework, writing a poem about slugs! Talking of which, the useless Simon has been no use at all on the domestic front whilst yours truly is on the road, trying to bring a smile to the hard-pressed mums of Britain and the world, according to my publishers!

Because, instead of writing a few simple lines about our slimy friends, Simon thinks it's more helpful to watch '100 Greatest Lift Music Classics' on the UK NBG Channel, presented by Paul Ross and A.A. Gill. So, guess who ended up having to write 'Ode To A Slug'? That's right, the private tutor we hired to help get Charlie into High Fees Pre-Preparatory School For Boys (the feeder for all the top prep schools which feed the top London day schools which feed all the top universities or, rather, they don't any more, which is a bloody disgrace when you've spent all that money, but that's another column!!).

SO, I hear you ask, what's the answer, Polly? How are you managing to launch an international best-seller (*'More Mummy For Old Rope'* – don't miss the author reading extracts at the Ashford Literary Festival, November 12th) with filling in the nightmare two weeks of Charlie's half-term?

Simple. Dump your offspring on your sister for the duration! She's got four kids (Rollo, Milo, Tizzy and Sprog), so she's hardly going to notice one more, not in a house that big! Meanwhile, the new Russian au-pair (Charlie calls her "Uzbecky" as a joke, since none of us can pronounce her real name) looks after Simon, allowing yours truly to further the cause of the Working Mum and rearrange the books in Waterstone's to make sure *'More Mummy For Old Rope'* is prominently displayed in front of some of the other, frankly, inferior "humorous" sideways looks at the perils of modern motherhood! (No offence to my rivals, ie *'Take The Mummy And Run'*, *'Funny Mummy'* and *'Mummy Makes The World Go Round'*, to name but three!?!)

© *P. Filler 2004.*

MANDY – THE TOAST OF BRUSSELS

That Astonishing Speech In Full

Bonjour matelots d'Europe!

Je suis 'Mandy', le plus fameux medicin de spin du monde.

Mais, ça c'est histoire.

Maintenant, je suis Mandy l'Européan!

Mandy, qui aime les croissants et le sauerkraut et les legendaire sprouts de Bruxelles!

Au Monsieur Blair et Madame Cherie je dis 'au revoir'!

Salut à Président Chirac et Chancellor Kohl et tous les autres, les noms de qui je ne souviens pas au moment! *(Consults notes)*

Ah, oui, et aussi salut à mon nouveau colleague, Président Barroso de Portugal!

Serieusement, mon agenda en Bruxelles est très simple!

A bas la corruption! A bas le sleaze! A bas la Grande Bretagne!

Vive l'Europe! Vive l'euro!

Vive moi-même!

Souvenez mon motto legendaire, 'Je ne suis pas un quitter, je suis un combatant!'

(An edited version of the new Trade Commissioner's address to the European Parliament can be read on the website www. mandyandreinaldogotobrussels.eu.int)

That All-Purpose Editorial In Full

OUR HEARTS go out to _____ and their family. The whole nation has joined together in collective grief for _____ and our thoughts and prayers are with _____. In churches across the country, candles were lit as the country came to terms with the tragedy of _____. Tributes of flowers were laid outside the home of _____ and there was a two-minute silence in football grounds everywhere. Surely it is time for a lasting memorial to _____ to be erected at public expense, possibly in the form of a fountain or a statue on the fourth plinth. Whatever happens, _____ must not be forgotten.

Tomorrow: Someone else.

BILLY CONNOLLY DIES HORRIBLY
by Our Showbiz Staff

THE 62-year-old comedian Mr Billy Connolly, a former shipyard worker, last night died horribly on stage at the Apollo Theatre after making a joke about British hostage Ken Bigley.

A video of Mr Connolly's last moments in showbusiness was posted on the internet and showed a silver-haired Scotsman pleading for his professional life. His family said, "He had simply gone to the theatre to try and make some money. It's a tragedy".

LATE SWING TO BUSH
Lady Magnesia To Blame

*by Our Man In Clark County, **Lunchtime O'Hio***

TOP BRITISH historian Lady Magnesia Freelove was hailed by republicans last night as the saviour of President Bush's faltering attempt to win a second term in the White House.

A personal letter from Lady Magnesia to the voters of key swing state Clark County urged them to vote for Senator Kerry. The letter, first printed in the Guardian newspaper, is now credited with provoking a huge nationwide backlash in favour of the incumbent president, giving Bush a staggering 60 point landslide lead in the final days of campaigning.

That Letter In Full

Dear Little American Person,

I am sure you have heard of me and may even have read my many books – 'The Life of King Henry the Ninth', 'Mary Queen of Wales' and 'Elizabeth III', to name only four.

Anyway, what you mustn't do in your election is vote for that frightful, vulgar, Bush fellow. Instead, you must put your cross next to the nice Mr Kerry, whose wife is very charming and very rich – just like myself.

And now my husband Harold who, as you no doubt know, is the world's greatest writer, would like to add a little thought of his own:

"Tell fucking Bush to fuck off and disappear up his own fucking arse."

I think that is rather beautifully put, don't you?

Lady Magnesia Freelove, Historian and Mother of Six, Islington.

"We're moving to Amsterdam to get you into the School of Rembrandt catchment area"

Lives Of The Martyrs

No. 94 BROTHER BORIS

AND there was in those far-off times a holy man, who was known to the multitude only as Boris. His habits were frugal and he travelled everywhere on a humble bicycle, being shouted at by passers-by. Alas, one day, Brother Boris became possessed by a devil, and called down curses on all the good people of the City of Liverpool, who had been many days mourning one of their number who had been cruelly put to death by the Saracens.

Boris went into an high place and cried out, "Woe unto ye, ye people of Mersey. For you are a generation of whingers, filled with mawkish sentimentality and self-pity. Cripeth! Gadzooks! What a dreadful shower you are, by all that is holy!"

No sooner had these intemperate words been uttered by Brother Boris (written out for him as they had been by his fellow-scribe Brother Simon Heffer), than the people of Liverpool waxed wroth.

Which was singular, for it was known that not a single citizen of that fair city ever read the uplifting tracts penned by Brother Boris and his tiny band of co-religionists.

Then in turn did Boris's superior, Father Michael, Abbott of the Transylvanian Brethren, also wax wroth, and commanded his errant novice to do penance for his wicked utterances.

He ordered Brother Boris to don sackcloth and ashes and to make a journey to the distant city of Liverpool, some eighty leagues hence. All along the way, the good friar must flagellate himself with rolled up copies of the Spectator, until finally he must go from door to door, pleading for forgiveness from the good folk of Scouseland.

And when Brother Boris carried out the instructions of Father Michael, the good people opened their doors and said "Clear off! We don't know who you are you pasty-faced Southern git!"

And they sent him on his way a sadder and a wiser man (Surely some mistaketh? Ed.).

THE SCOUSTATOR
The Victim Culture

Whilst the sad events of recent days may tempt some to feel sympathy for the beleaguered staff of the *Spectator*, it is worth remembering that they have brought this tragedy upon their own heads, by deliberately fostering a culture based on a sense of social and moral superiority to the rest of society.

It is true that in recent years the *Spectator* has produced many celebrities who have been cultural icons of our time.

One thinks of such names as TV's Charles Moore, the top sexual athlete Rod Liddle, the beautiful Kimberley Fortier and, of course, the legendary Greek playboy Taki Takalotof-cokeupthenos.

But behind this veneer of cultural vitality lies a sorry picture of drunkenness, laziness and an arrogant belief that the world owes them a living.

To be frank, the inhabitants of 56 Doughty Street are a bunch of sad, incompetent tossers who (Cont. p. 94)

'I MUST CHOOSE' admits TV's Boris

by Our Spectator Staff **Christopher Housemaster**

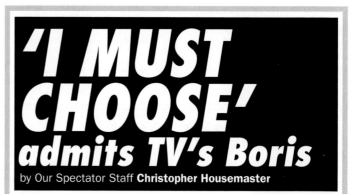

BORIS JOHNSON, the MP for Henley and editor of the Spectator, has admitted that he faces a difficult choice in his busy career.

"I have been trying to do two things at once and I now accept that I have to make a choice between being a buffoon or being a twit. You can't do both."

Said a close friend, "I think Boris will pack in being a twit and concentrate on the buffoonery. Don't forget he's very ambitious and secretly harbours a desire to be leader of the (Cont. p. 94)

LIVERPOOL FURY OVER VICTIM MENTALITY SLUR

WORLD LEADERS CONGRATULATE BUSH

ONCE IT became clear that George Bush had won a second term, world leaders immediately rang the President to congratulate him.

"Within minutes the President's closest friends in the international community were all on the phone, with Tony Blair, Vladimir Putin, Gerhard Schroeder and Osama bin Laden offering their heartfelt congratulations," said a senior White House *(cont. p. 94)*

LATE KERRY NEWS

JOHN KERRY says that following his election defeat, he plans to retire from politics and return to his family business.

"I'm looking forward to returning to my Easter Island home and resuming work there as a statue."

My eBay

i'mnumberone! (2)

Items I'm Selling (1-5 of 5 items)

	Current Price	Postage Cost	Bids
☐ **Flip-flops – men's, size 12**			
	$9.99	$2.50	0
☐ **Job lot – assorted rosettes, balloons, etc – inc. 4 tonnes tickertape**			
	$199.99	buyer to collect	0
☐ **Pocket calculator – some wear – needs new battery**			
	$5.99	$2.00	0
☐ **Rabbit's foot charm**			
	$1.99	$1.99	0
☐ **'The West Wing' DVD – seasons 1-3 – unwanted gift**			
	$9.99	$7.50	0

"He died of exhaustion looking for his car keys"

Peel Collection For British Library

Culture Minister Hails 'Historic Bequest'

by Our Arts Correspondent "D.J." Taylor

NOT SINCE it acquired the Elgin Marbles in the 19th Century has the British Museum received such a priceless bequest as the gift, announced yesterday, of the unique collection of CDs and vinyls assembled over the years by one of the greatest cultural figures of the 20th Century, the late John Peel.

When Mr Peel died last month, tributes to his lifetime of artistic achievement poured in from every corner of the globe, praising his unique sense of musical taste and his unerring instinct for identifying every

major music-al movement of the twen-tieth century – punk, funk, junk, hip-hop, flip-flop, slip-slop, garage, council house, indie, daily telegraph, dance, trance, pot, shit, fusion, fission, fashion and, of course, spam.

The Peel Archive, which now runs to some 25 million separate musical items, includes some of the rarest recordings in the entire history of music. Among them are:

■ the 1962 demo pressing of *Ton-Up Kid* by Tom and the Tom Men

■ the 1968 Kaleidoscope Dreamscape album by the Exploding Yoghurt Band, which only sold one copy

■ 1977, *Fuckya* by Sadie Nix & The Nickers, which Peel was the first DJ to promote against stiff opposition from BBC bosses

■ 1987, The Techno Monks of Hilversum Abbey with their plainsong arrangement of Geoffrey de Bindman's *Te Deum* with a drum-and-bass backing.

(That's enough terrible records. Ed.)

Forgotten Royal Dies

by Hugh Montgomery-Massivesnob

The Duchess at the Coronation (arrowed)

PRINCESS Marjorie Lavinia Aloysia Starborgling of Worcester died today, aged 138.

She was the youngest of 13 daughters to the 5th Earl of Pangbourne, and a grand-niece of Queen Adelaide, the second cousin of Queen Victoria.

In 1908, the then Lady Marjorie Starborgling married Prince Cecil, Duke of Worcester, in a glittering society wedding at St Margaret's, Westminster, described by the Morning Post as "the most glittering society wedding of the century".

At the reception afterwards, the guest list included every crowned head in Europe and the cream of the Edwardian aristocracy, headed by the Dukes of Hertfordshire, Herefordshire and Hampshire, and the Dowager Marchioness of Dorking *(Get on with the story. Ed.)*

Intensely shy and reserved, Princess Marjorie never played a leading role in society herself, preferring as she did to remain in her beloved garden at Brooms, where for many years she cultivated a large area of grass which she called her "beloved lawn".

In later years she developed a keen interest in antique fountain pens, amassing a collection which filled several rooms in the East Wing of her husband's baronial mansion in Glenmorangie.

In 1921 she made a rare departure from her customary life of solitude when she paid an informal royal visit to the Gambia, where she was received by the Governor, Sir Archibald Pontefract-Starborgling, a distant relative of her husband.

Together they made a sporting foray into the jungle, where Sir Archibald shot a record number of tree-dwelling meerkats. A picture of this historic achievement was later published in the *Illustrated London News* under the heading 'Princess Sees Record Bag By Governor'.

She recorded the event in her diary (as yet unpublished) in the following memorable passage:

"June 15. Frightfully warm for the time of year. Archie says he has a real treat in store for me today. I am to be allowed to watch him shoot meerkat. Most enjoyable. Went to bed early with a slight headache."

After the death of her beloved husband in 1938, Princess Marjorie became something of a recluse, shunning the limelight which other members of the Royal Family were not loath to embrace.

In 1960 she made a visit to Harrods, where she was greeted by the then manager Mr Smidgett, who mistook her for the Queen Mother.

"Don't worry," she wittily riposted. "People are always doing that." She often regaled visitors to Brooms with this story in later years, to general hilarity.

Perhaps her greatest achievement in an age when Royalty was to become almost synonymous with gossip was to remain entirely free from any breath of scandal.

Through many decades her name was never mentioned in the press, a fact which delighted her to the point where she would collect newspapers in which she had not been mentioned, as proof of her dedication to her royal duty.

She did, however, attract a paragraph in the *Evesham & Pershore Evening Echo* when she donated her fountain pen collection to the local Museum of the Written Word (formerly the Sackville-West Moth Museum).

On hearing of her death yesterday, one acquaintance said *(contd p. 94)*

Another Extraordinary Day For An Extraordinary Newspaper

Dear Times Reader,

Since it was first launched in 1788, the Times has maintained a long and distinguished tradition as a newspaper of record and as a byword for journalistic integrity.

It was in keeping with that historic and noble spirit that has always characterised the Times of London that we assured you that we would never abandon the Broadsheet edition of our great newspaper. Indeed, we made a solemn and binding promise to this effect.

We have now decided to do exactly the opposite and to go entirely tabloid. Many of you may feel betrayed by this decision, but we would ask you all to remember that we don't care and that you can get stuffed.

Yours faithfully

Robert Thomson

(dictated in his absence by the proprietor, Rupert Murdoch, aka The Dirty Fibber)

"Apparently the deceased was a great party-giver"

IT'S THE NEW BAND AID

♫ Do they know who we are? ♫

The Queen's Speech

What Her Majesty's Government plans to ban in the coming session:

☐ A Bill to outlaw smacking in pubs and offices

☐ A Bill to outlaw smoking with dogs

☐ A Bill to outlaw smirking at frogs
(under the EU's Racial Discrimination and
Inflammatory Practices directive, 2004/29)

☐ A Bill to outlaw smoking in bogs, unless you are a
consenting member of the Gay Community

☐ A Bill to permit "responsible" gambling in public
toilets with dogs

(That's enough Bills. Ed.)

HOON WILL BE OVER BY CHRISTMAS
Government New Pledge

by Our Defence Staff **Phil Coffins**

THE PRIME Minister has promised that, come what may, the Defence Secretary, Geoff Hoon, will be withdrawn by Christmas.

"Hoon has been in the front line over Iraq, taking flak from all sides," said the Prime Minister.

Black Death

"The least we can do is bring him home for Christmas to spend time with his family."

However, angry relatives of Mr Hoon said, "He should never have been there in the first place. He is totally ill-equipped for this type of action."

Fall-ujah guy

They continued, "Anyway, we do not believe this assurance from the Prime Minister. He has promised before to relieve him of his duties, but Geoff is still there on the front line being sniped at".

"You're right, it is a big ask..."

That Kinnock Maiden Speech In Full

Lord Kinnochio of Windbag:
My Lords, Ladies and Lords. Pray silence for myself. And let me begin by totally and utterly refuting the claims which have been in the Tory press that I have at any time sought in any manner, shape or form, to abolish Your Lordships' chamber, which is a total and utter lie, as is any suggestion that I ever described your lordships and ladyships as a "bunch of clapped-out geriatric spongers who should all be strung-up." Because what I totally and utterly said was that my admiration for this noble and ancient house was utterly total and totally utter". And furthermore that throughout my long and distinguished life in public service my constant and unwavering dream has been that one day I should be privileged to take my seat in this historic chamber, redolent as it is of the rich tapestry which has bound

these island peoples together for centuries past. And today I say to you, this is not the end of my maiden speech. It is not even the end of the beginning. But it is the begining of the end of the begining which I must...

All Noble Lords: Shut up, you old windbag, get back to Brussels. Some of us are trying to get some sleep.
© *Hanz-z-z-z-ard*

PRINCE CHARLES IN 'ABOVE STATION' ROW

by Our Royal Staff **Paul Maul**

THE Prince of Wales was plunged into the centre of a major new controversy when an extraordinary memo was revealed, claiming that he was expecting "to be promoted above his capabilities".

The secret memo, which is believed to have come from Her Majesty The Queen, came to light when the Prince protested about his conditions of employment.

An exasperated monarch wrote to her private secretary, Sir

Michael Gropetrouser:

What is wrong with young people nowadays?

"They seem to think that, just because they got a few 'O' levels and went to Cambridge, they can lecture us all on how the country should be run. They bang on in their PC way about the environment, GM crops and global warming as if they knew something about it. They even, I gather, imagine that one day they can walk into the highest positions in the land, even though such a job is way beyond their abilities. One really does not know what the world is coming to.

Signed
H.M. The Queen

■ **Should Charles be sacked, or is the Queen guilty of discriminating against him?**

Now you too can join the debate at www.sackchazza.com

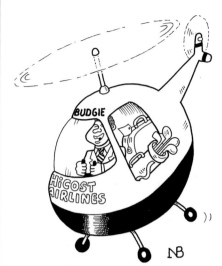

MODERN NURSERY RHYMES

The grand young Duke of York,
He wouldn't go by train.
He flew up North for a round of golf,
And he flew back down again.

Rub-a-dub-dub,
Three men in a pub
Can't have a fag if
it also serves grub.

What are little girls made of?
Cuppa-Soups and Hula-Hoops –
That's what little girls are made of.

What are little boys made of?
Oven chips and chicken dips –
That's what little boys are made of.

Lines Written On The Dismissal As Culture Spokesman To The Conservative Party Of Mr Boris Johnson, MP For Henley-on-Thames

By William Rees-McGonagall

'Twas in the Year Of Our Lord Two Thousand and Four
That the famous Boris Johnson was shown the door.
He who had so proudly sat on the Tory front bench
Now had to step down amid a terrible stench.

Only weeks before this young Etonian fop
Had been tipped to rise to the very top.
With his tousled hair and crumpled suits,
They said he alone could fill Mrs Thatcher's boots.

He was the nation's favourite Tory
Until the gutter press revealed a most unfortunate story.
It turned out that this charming and likeable fella
Had formed an extra-marital liaison with a lady named Petronella.

When the hacks besieged his home to put Boris on the spot,
He rashly told them "Cripes! This is all piffle and rot."
The same story he repeated to his leader, Mr Howard,
Because, to be honest, he was a wee bit of a coward.

As the story exploded, Boris continued to deny it,
But he had reckoned without Petronella's mother, Lady Verushka Wyatt.
Thus it was that the downfall of the editor of the *Spectator*
Was caused by none other than his mistress's mater.

She was only too happy to give the hacks their head
By telling them that Boris had promised her daughter to wed
And, as if that in itself was not enough
He had also got poor Petsy up the duff.

And, to continue with this sordid recitation,
Boris had insisted on a termination.
But when there arose the little matter of the bill,
He exclaimed, "I can't pay that! Perhaps your mother will."

When Michael Howard read this squalid tale,
Recounted over 20 pages of the *Sunday Mail,*
He felt that Boris had taken him for a ride.
"I trusted him," he said, "and the scoundrel lied."

So Howard furiously picked up the phone
And waited as he listened to the ringing tone.
When Boris answered, "Michael, can I ring you back?"
He was told, "No, you can't, Boris – I'm giving you the sack."

"I don't mind how many women you have had,
Nor whether your treatment of them has been appallingly bad.
The one thing I as leader cannot abide
Is that one of my front-bench spokesmen has lied."

For Boris, it was the end of a glittering career
And throughout the nation there was many a tear.
Said Boris, "I've been a chump, and an ass and a twit."
Though the phrase he was looking for was "total (cont'd p. 94)

Those All-Purpose Boris Columns In Full

IT'S THE WIFE I FEEL SORRY FOR

by **Philippa Column**

IT'S THE wife I feel sorry for. To be publicly humiliated by your husband and to have to read about his infidelity in the papers must be difficult to bear. And the worst thing of all must be the pieces saying "It's the wife I feel sorry for", constantly reminding people that she has been publicly humiliated by her husband and forcing her to read about his infidelity.

Make no mistake, being pitied by newspaper columnists must make you feel completely worthless. As I say, it's the wife I feel sorry for (cont. p. 94)

WHAT'S ALL THE FUSS ABOUT?

by **Phil Space**

WHAT's all the fuss about? OK, so his private life is a bit of a mess. But it's none of our business and the press has no right to go on about it. The fact that he got his mistress pregnant, betrayed his wife and four children and lied to his boss should not be dredged up in the newspapers just to titillate their readers.

None of this has any bearing on his ability to carry out his public duties.

The love-romps, the abortions, the lies – these should not even merit discussion and are certainly not subjects for prurient press comment.

As I say, "What's all the fuss about?"

> To have one abortion, Mr Johnson, may be regarded as a misfortune; to have two looks like carelessness

Lady Wyatt in "The Importance of Being Boris" Act 1, Scene 3

That Budd Report In Full

**To The Prime Minister
From Sir Zola Budd QCMG, QT, QED**

An Investigation Into Allegations Surrounding The Conduct Of The Home Secretary, the Rt. Hon. David Blunkett R.C., M.P.

1.1 As an old friend of the Home Secretary, I was asked by the Prime Minister to carry out a full inquiry into the issuing of permanent UK resident's status to Miss Philippina Philippino of the Philippines.

1.2 After giving this matter very careful consideration, I have concluded that Mr Blunkett's conduct in this matter is not within the remit of my inquiry.

1.3 This is because such an investigation might indicate that Mr Blunkett may in some way have behaved in an inappropriate manner, which he clearly hasn't, as I have already been informed at the very highest level (by the Prime Minister).

1.4 In the light of the above, I am fully satisfied that the Home Secretary has at all times behaved with the utmost propriety, in keeping with his high office. And if he hasn't, it is none of my business.

Signed
*Lord Budd of Whitewash,
Master of Hutton College,
The University of Butler.*

Great Moments In Comedy

To father one child by someone else's wife, Mr Blunkett, might be considered a misfortune. To father two looks like carelessness

"The Importance of Being Honest" Act 1

"We should never have let him go to that art school"

Hunting With Dogs To Be Banned

with '**Old Shagger**'

THE AGE-OLD sport of hunting women with a dog is to be outlawed under new legislation rushed through by the prime minister yesterday.

A leading campaigner, Mr Stephen Quinn, said, "In this day and age it is outrageous that Home Secretaries should be allowed to roam the country with their dog, trying to sniff out women whom they can then jump on and maul."

Blunking With Dogs

"If you have ever been in at 'the kill', it is a disgusting spectacle," Mr Quinn concluded, "and would put you off this so-called sport for life."

However, a leading enthusiast for the sport, a Mr D.N.A. Blunkett (no relation unless proved to the contrary), was strongly opposed to the ban.

Foxy Lady

"There is no finer sight than a Home Secretary and his dog in full cry, as they pursue their quarry into the nearest wood.

"If all this must now come to an end, it would be a very sad day. I may even have to face the prospect of losing my job."

NEW ENGLISH PROVERBS

"THE SHIT HITS THE TAN"

EU CHIEF DEFENDS NEW TEAM

by Our Brussels Correspondent **Jacques Tatty**

EUROPEAN president Jose Manuel Barroso has defended his decision to appoint a convicted criminal as the EU's new transport commissioner.

"Jacques Barrot's experience will be invaluable to the commission," insisted Mr Barroso. "And I'm stuck with him *[Surely "sticking with him"? Ed.]* 100 percent."

Egg and Cresson face

Mr Barrot, found guilty of embezzling party funds in his native France, failed to tell the commission about his conviction.

"But the important thing is he got away with it – as he did with the original crime, thanks to a pardon from President Chirac," said Mr Barroso.

Mr Barrot isn't the only appointment to cause a furore. Earlier, Italy's Rocco Buttiglione had to stand down as justice commissioner when it emerged he had a string of convictions as a Roman Catholic.

"If he'd had convictions for fraud or lying on his mortgage application form, it might have been different," said one Labour *MEP.* "But he believes *(cont. p. 94)*

SEX EMPORIUM

POLLY FILLER'S CHRISTMAS ROUND ROBIN

Dear everyone,

It's been quite a year for the Filler family, with Polly's best-selling book *Mummy For Old Rope* storming the best-seller lists on both sides of the Atlantic(!), not to mention the Pacific and the Mediterranean(!!!).

In April, Polly heard that *Mummy For Old Rope* (£7.99) was to be made into a hugely successful Hollywood film, with Scarlett Johansson playing Polly! The director – somebody or other called Sam Mendes(!!!) – wasn't sure that Scarlett was good-looking enough, but since Polly is too busy working on the sequel *Mummy Doesn't Grow On Trees!*, she will have to do!

Toddler Charlie continues to dazzle his teachers, who think he is a prodigy, but I say that a reading age of 25 when you are three-and-a-half is par for the course in the Filler family!

I won't go on about his grade eight violin, lead in the school play, captaincy of the soccer, rugger and debating teams, or his conditional place at Oxford because we don't want him to get big-headed!! Not that he would, because everyone says he is the most lovely, funny child they have ever met and so like his mum!

Meanwhile, the Useless Simon has had a particularly useless year, mostly lying around in front of his new plasma screen television, watching 'Jeremy Clarkson Test Drives A Smart Bomb' on BBC 94. When he wasn't doing that he was out at the Sports Bar watching Pro Celebrity Sex Change, introduced by A.A. Gill and Paul Ross on the Sky Nasty Channel!

2004 proved a record year for au-pairs as we went through 27 – in one month! Our latest has selfishly deserted us for Christmas, returning to her home in Sudan to look for her missing relatives. Well, more fool Darfuria because she's going to miss the best Christmas ever!

Oh, and my parents died.

Wishing you all a Happy Christmas and a Filler-tastic 2005!

Polly, Useless Simon & Charlie

MESSAGE OF CHRISTMAS 'FORGOTTEN'

by Our Religious Staff
Tesc O'Booze and Terry Waitrose

HAS the Britain of today lost touch with the essential meaning of Christmas?

Judging by the evidence of the past month, the answer is tragically 'yes'.

In times past, the whole nation would join together in a celebration of spending.

The Lolly and the Gravy

High streets and shopping malls were packed to bursting, with happy families merrily handing over stacks of money to fill their car boots with piles of gifts that symbolised the ancient meaning of Christmas.

But this year, in what was described as "the worst Christmas ever", attendances at shops declined to a record low level.

Only a few elderly people were still prepared to brave the overheated supermarkets in their attempt to keep alive the spirit of what Christmas used to be all about.

The disheartened chairman of one retail chain said last night, "It is all very sad. No longer can it be said that we are a shop-going nation. Children grow up these days without any concept of the central part that Christmas shop-attendance used to play in our national life."

Daily Telegraph Christmas 🎄 Appeal 🎄

AT THIS season of charity and goodwill, our thoughts naturally turn to all those who are less fortunate than ourselves – above all, the hapless victims of cruelty and injustice. We think, in particular, this Christmas of two twin brothers incarcerated in their island prison who find themselves faced, through no fault of their own, with a massive bill for libel damages and costs, due to the incompetence of Lord Black and the staff of the *Daily Telegraph*.

If you wish to contribute you can phone your donation personally to any of these famous *Daily Telegraph* contributors:

BILL DEEDES, the world's oldest man

BORIS JOHNSON, the fun-loving former shadow minister for whatever it was

CHARLES MOORE, who wishes to make it clear that he was on holiday at the time when the offending piece about Mr Galloway was published

WAS A REALITY TV STAR 15 MINUTES AGO

GLENDA SLAGG

THE GIRL IN THE SACK!

■ DIDN'T your heart go out to poor Davy Blunkett as he opened his soul to the nation and told us how much he loved his little lad!!?!? I'm a hard-bitten hackette, but let me tell you, mister, even I shed a tear – no, what am I saying, I wept buckets as this dear, sweet daddy poured out his troubles on the telly??!? David, we didn't deserve you!!!?! Boo hoo hoo!!!

■ DAVID BLUNKETT!!?! Didn't he make you sick??!?? Taking out the onion and turning on the waterworks!?!? Come off it, you bearded baby, the only person *you* were crying for was yourself!!??! I'm a soft-centred, sentimental gal, but let me tell you, mister, even I had a lump in my throat – no, what am I saying??!??! I vomited buckets at the sight of you trying to spin your tawdry tale on the telly!!????!

David, you deserved what you got!??! And then some!!! Urgh?!? Urgh!!!?

■ *AND HERE is the Ten O'Clock News!!??! Bonk!!! Sir Trevor MacDonald's Marriage In Crisis!!?! Bonk!!! Trevor Having Trial Separation!!??! Bonk!!?! Trevor Being Comforted By Younger Woman!!??!* (You're fired. Ed.)

■ HERE they are – Glenda's Yuletime Yummies:

● Father Christmas – OK, so he's old and bearded!?! It didn't stop Kimberly Fortier!!?! Geddit???!?

● Rudolph The Red-Nosed Reindeer – OK, so you've got a shiny nose!??! What else you got, Rudy??!??

● The Snowman – I'll warm you up, big boy, and you'll melt in my arms!!!?!? *(You really are fired. Ed.)*

Byeeee!!!

Like me new bag and boots? Phil got 'em for me!

NEW-LOOK QUEEN

"Yes, now we're using Bobski The Builder – SO much cheaper"

IN THE COURTS
Galloway v. The Daily Torygraph Day 94

Before Mr Justice E.D. Cocklecarrot

(Mr Galloway continued to give evidence under examination from his counsel Sir Ephraim Hugefee Q.C.)

Sir Ephraim *(for it is he)*: Mr Gallowglass, what was your reaction when you read in an editorial in the Daily Telegraph that you had been a traitor to your country and that, in the words of the leader-writer, you should be "strung up", for it was the only language that you understood?

Mr Gallowtree: It was like a poisoned arrow piercing my heart. It was like a scimitar slicing through my soul. It was like an Arab dagger penetrating to the very entrails of my being...

Cocklecarrot: Yes, I think we've got the general idea.

Mr Gallopingmajor: Your Honour, I am but a humble Scottish crofter from the slums of the Gorbals. I have not enjoyed the advantages of an expensive education like your good self. All I have to survive on is this humble onion.

(Mr Galloway, at this point, took out a vegetable of the type described above and began to weep copiously. Mr Topp-Price Q.C. for the Daily Telegraph then began his cross-examination of the plaintiff.)

Mr Topp-Price: Mr McTraitor, I ask you to look at this photograph of a luxury villa on the Costa Fortune in Portugal. I put it to you, Mr McHaw-Haw, that as a humble MP the only way you could have afforded to purchase such a property was if you were in receipt of several million barrels of oil given to you by your good friend Saddam Husssein.

Mr Galleyslave: How dare you, you soft Sassenach bastard. You come outside and I'll break your heed.

Cocklecarrot: Please calm down, Mr McLooney. Mr Topp-Price was not accusing you of anti-semitism.

Mr Galilee: This is an outrage equivalent to genocide. How dare anyone mention anti-semitism in my presence. I would like to make clear that I have never smoked a cigar in my life, let alone one given to me by the late Chairman Arafat, as you allege.

Mr Topp-Price *(producing picture of Mr Galloway smoking large Havana cigar)*: I draw your attention to this photograph of yourself published in the Torygraph under the heading 'Liar, Liar, Your Cigar's On Fire'. How do you account for that, Mr Galway-Bay?

Mr Galloping-Consumption: The document is a fake. Any fool can see that. Even to look at it sends a poisoned dart into my bowels, and...

Cocklecarrot *(waking up)*: Haven't we had this bit already?

(After a break for luncheon at the Garrick, Mr Justice Cocklecarrot returned to hear legal arguments on behalf of the Daily Libelgraph.)

Sir Price Waterhouse Q.C.: My Lord, we intend in this case to offer the defence known as *Non Legum Standi*. I refer you to the case of Reynolds v. the Funday Times, where the paper was able to show, successfully, that although what they had printed was patently untrue, the very fact that it had entertained the readers should be regarded as justification and as serving the national interest. I refer, of course, Your Honour, to Q13.VIII.43, a copy of which you will find in your bundle.

Cocklecarrot: I am indebted to you, Mr Topp-Price, I see here a number of documents in what appears to be an Arabic script. Do these also have some bearing on this case?

Mr Topp-Price: These are the original documents discovered in a shoe box in Baghdad, which prove that Mr Gallowtree was in receipt of billions of barrels of oil from Mr Hussein. Or possibly not.

Cocklecarrot: Forgive me, but is that not the whole point of this case?

Mr Topp-Price: We submit, My Lord, that it is not, and that with respect, Your Honour, you have failed fully to grasp the principle of *Non Legum Standi*, on which our defence rests. Perhaps I could explain it to you later over a drink at the Garrick.

(Later a film was shown of Mr Galway-Bay prostrating himself before Saddam Hussein and kissing his shoes, while uttering the words, "I salute you, O noble warrior and ruler of the desert sands.")

Mr Topp-Price: Would you not say, Mr Gorbals, that this video provides irrefutable proof that you were a lickspittle of the late dictator, and a craven apologist for the world's most evil man?

Mr Galtieri: This is ridiculous. That video was taken wholly out of context. My words were wrongly translated from the original Scottish. What I actually said was, "You are a ruthless despot, of the type I oppose with every fibre of my being." To see my words twisted in this way strikes a poisoned dagger into the very seat of my soul, it...

Cocklecarrot: Do we have to have this again? Can't we call Charles Moore instead? He lives down my way, you know. Seems like a thoroughly decent chap.

(Counsel then explained that Mr Moore, although the editor of the time, had spent the day in question on the hunting field, leaving the paper in the capable hands of his subordinate, Mr Derbyshire, and that therefore he, Mr Moore, would not be giving evidence in person, owing to an important lunch at the Savoy Grill.)

The case continues...

The last time I saw Dad he was on TV, wearing a Batman suit, standing on a ledge at Buckingham Palace...

HUNTER apols W.F.YEAMES

CRUISE SHOCK

Would you do me the honour of being my next ex-wife?

POETRY CORNER

Lines on the retirement of Michael Fish, meteorologist

So. Farewell then
Michael Fish.
Famous for forecasting
The weather
For 30 years.

Your most celebrated
Prediction of course
Was that there would
Not be
A hurricane.

But there was.

So can we believe you
When you predict
Your imminent
Retirement?

We might turn on
The news and find
You are still
There.

E.J. Thribb (17½
– or 93º Fahrenheit)

In Memoriam Françoise Sagan

So. Farewell
Then.
Françoise Sagan.
Famous author
of Bonjour
Tristesse.

How ironic
That seems
Today now
That you have
Passed on.

E.J. Thribb (17½)

In Memoriam Strawberry Fields

So. Farewell
Then Strawberry
Fields –

The Liverpool
Children's home
Made famous
By the Beatles'
Song.

"Strawberry Fields
Forever."

Except you
Weren't.

E.J. Thribb (17½)

THE SABBATH TIMES

Friday, January 7, 2005 — 2 Shekels

Flood Catastrophe Latest

WORST DISASTER IN HISTORY OF WORLD

Many Britons Feared Dead

by Our Man on the Ark **Noah**

FOLLOWING the greatest flood the world has ever known, fears were mounting last night that many British citizens may have perished in the huge natural catastrophe that has over-taken the entire globe.

As I look out from the crowded deck of the ark, writes *Sabbath Times* man Noah, it has become increasingly clear that everyone in the world except me has been washed away by the unprecedented rise in sea levels.

This leads me to the horrifying conclusion that the death toll is likely to include many Britons, possibly all of them.

'I Blame God'

Says Top Sabbath Times Columnist, Ham

AS THE full scale of the catastrophe which has wiped out mankind began to sink in yesterday, attention began to focus on the mysterious figure who is believed to have been responsible for the flood.

I can reveal that the 'Deluge' was not a freak act of nature, as some have claimed, but a carefully orchestrated act of God.

Questions are already being asked at the highest level – well, nearly at the highest level – as to why the so-called Almighty caused the flood to happen, fully aware that it would lead to widespread loss of life.

And why was there no warning of the disaster? Last night this was denied by a spokesman for God, my father Noah.

Speaking from the bridge of the Ark, at a press conference attended by myself and my brothers Shem and Japheth, Noah claimed that "mankind was given ample warning, as it happens. I myself issued a number of weather forecasts, predicting continuous rain for forty days.

"But mankind was too busy whoring after strange gods."

Profile

The Great Survivor

WHO is he, the only man in the world left alive? Noah, 81, is a tall, distinguished, bearded man, with a lifelong interest in animal welfare and DIY.

Happily married, with a wife and three sons, he *(cont. p. 94)*

HUNTER

BUSH SLAMS 'ACT OF TERROR'

by Our Political Staff **Eartha Quake**

THE President of the United States today hit out at those responsible for what he called "the worst terrorist outrage since 9/11".

He told a White House press conference, "We don't yet know who these tsunami guys are, but I tell you, we will hunt them down to the end of the earth".

CORRECTION

The President later issued a clarification, claiming that he had been misquoted by himself.

"What the President intended to say," explained his press secretary Myra Gaffe, "was that he is promising free and fair elections in Tsunamia as soon as he can find it on the map."

'I BLAME NO ONE'

Says No One

by Our Scientific Staff **Phil Space**

IN THE wake of the worst natural disaster for half a century, no one today decided that the main person to blame was no one.

However, a spokesman was quick to refute these claims, saying "It must be someone's fault, surely? What about the Archbishop of Canterbury? I blame him for *(cont. p. 94)*

HUGE WAVE OF MONEY FAILS TO ENGULF DISASTER ZONES

by Our Catastrophe Staff **Sue Nami**

A WORLDWIDE wave of money officially pledged by hundreds of governments yesterday failed to reach the stricken areas of Asia.

Said one onlooker in the Thai resort of Phukall, "The wave was tiny. Just a few million pounds. It's a disaster. We're just waiting here on the beach hoping for the big wave of money given by ordinary individuals to arrive, since the governmental response has *(cont. p94)*

Daily Mail

Tsunami Special

AREN'T WE MARVELLOUS?

by **Our Entire Staff**

THE GREAT news coming out of the admittedly sad Indian Ocean disaster is that the Daily Mail Flood Appeal is a huge success.

Loads of ordinary Daily Mail readers are giving money to our Daily Mail Appeal (rather than just giving it to the charities direct) and, even better, lots of celebrities are very generously allowing us to put their names on the front page of the Daily Mail in return for a donation. So, hats off to ourselves at the Daily Mail for our amazing self-promotion *(surely selflessness?)*.

ON OTHER PAGES ● **Is there a God?** Celebs ask the Big Question! **12** ● **Will the Tsunami cause House Prices to Fall? 94**

"Josh, wake up – we can't work the DVD player"

KNACKER BACKS 'SHOOT TO KILL' CAMPAIGN

by Our Crime Staff **Dominic Longarmofthelawson**

CHIEF INSPECTOR 'Knacker of the Yard' Knacker today gave his support to householders who take the law into their own hands and kill intruders.

Said Knacker: "For too long people have expected the police to come round and help them during burglaries. This is a waste of police time, when our officers could be better occupied doing their paperwork or picking up their takeaway curries ("chicken madras, poppadoms, no lager thanks I'm on duty, oh, all right, just the one").

Knacker, who retires this year, said that he was keen for the public to share the burden of law enforcement with uniformed officers.

"The way to cut crime in this country is for ordinary citizens to carry guns at all times and to exercise their right to shoot anybody who might be about to commit a crime."

Sir John Knacker is 94.

ON OTHER PAGES

INSPECTOR Knacker is to investigate claims that M. Henri Paul, the late Princess Diana's chauffeur, was in fact employed by aliens who were attempting to abduct her and take her to Venus to start a new colony of superbeings. He would like to talk confidentially to any aliens who might have any relevant information. He can be contacted at the Fugger Suite at the Ritz in Paris during office hours.

What You Didn't Hear Radio 4

The News Quiz, 12.27am
(Silly music)

Voiceover: ...and here's your chairman, Simon Hoggart!
(Applause)

Hoggart: Which journalist this week **hogg**-ed the limelight and made an **art** of himself? Alan?

Coren: Is this the one about the one-legged zebra that escaped from the zoo?

Hoggart: No, it isn't.

Francis Wheen *(for it is he)*: Is it the one about you getting your leg over...?

Hoggart: Well, that's all we've got time for this week.
(Silly music. Ends)

I'm not Deayton yet!

"Maybe doing a nude calendar isn't the best way of helping the tsunami victims..."

Yes! It's your guide to the socio-economic group that everyone is talking about

THE DAVS

What is a "Dav"?

DAV is an abbreviation of "David Thomas" and it stands for huge space-filling articles about Chavs to show how amusing the working classes are.

What are typical Dav names?

David and Thomas.

Where can we see Davs?

Everyday in the Daily Mail of course, generally opposite the editorial but sometimes next to the feature about kittens who look like Hitler.

What does a Dav look like?

They are prematurely bald and wear designer glasses.

How common are Davs?

Not at all common. They went to Eton and are furious that they are not quite as rich as Wayne Rooney.

Do Davs wear big checks?

No they carry them to the bank.

© *Daily Thomas of the Daily Mail*

GRAND SPECTATOR NEW YEAR COMPETITION

WHO do you think is the famous "Fifth Man"?

The names of four of Kimberly Quinn's lovers have already been identified. But who was the fifth?

And, indeed, the sixth, the seventh or the eighth?

 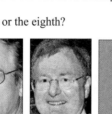 

Is it:
a) Boris Johnson
b) Lord Weidenfeld
c) TV's Charles Moore
d) Tony Blair
e) Bernie Ecclestone
f) Mike Gatting
g) Paul Burrell
h) Imran Khan
i) Lord Hutton
j) Jamie Oliver
k) Brian Sewell

Winner gets a year's subscription to the Spectator! Runner-up gets two years subscription to the Spectator!!

New Words

Hoggart (n): an unlikely or improbable lover. "That boring-looking man in the glasses is her hoggart" *(The Siege of Kimberly, 1879)*

Hoggart (vb): to issue violent denials of something that turns out to be true (see hogwash). "He tried to hoggart his way out of it, but his wife wasn't fooled for a moment" *(The Spectators, C.P. Snow, 1954)*

Hoggarts (proper noun): fictional school for wizards, where pupils learn to conjure up articles out of nothing, mocking politicians for their sexual foibles. *(Taken from Harry Potter And The Guardian of Humbug, 2002)*

HOON ANNOUNCES NEW-LOOK SCOTTISH ARMY

by Our Lack of Defence Staff **M.O.D. Cuts**

IN A shock announcement last night Geoffrey Hoon unveiled his plans for an amalgamation of all the Scottish regiments into "a slimmed-down agile fighting elite" to be renamed "The King's Own Black Watch Argyll and Highlander Royal Scots Fusiliers" – or "Hamish" for short.

The new regiment will have:

- One tartan
- One cap badge
- One rifle
- One soldier ("Hamish")

Fighting Farce

Said Mr Hoon: "I am confident that this is the way forward in a world fraught with the threat of terrorism where ground troops are more and more vital for the security of the nation."

POETRY CORNER

In Memoriam Cyril Fletcher

So. Farewell
Then. Cyril
Fletcher.
Famous poet,
Comedian and
Star of
"That's Life".

"I've got a
Cutting for you,
Esther."
Yes, that
Was your catchphrase.

I have a
Cutting here that
Says "Cyril Fletcher
Has Died".

That's Death!
(My odd ode
For this
Week.)

E.J. Thribb (17½)

In Memoriam Tommy Vance, Disc Jockey

So. Farewell
Then Tommy
Vance –
The Voice
Of Rock.

You were christened
Richard Anthony
Crispian Francis
Prue
Hope-West.

"Hi there. This
Is the Richard
Anthony Crispian
Francis Prue
Hope-West
Show!"

No. This
Would not
Have sounded
So good on Radio
One.

E.J. Thribb (17½)

This poem has been entered for the Whitbread Young Poet Of The Year Prize (Judges: Andrew Motion, Zachariah Zulu, and a man with a beard).

ALTERNATIVE HISTORY

"I chopped the cherry tree down, father, because it was potentially dangerous"

"It's time to put this behind us now and move on"

GIN LANE

"Once we get round-the-clock drinking, all this will sort itself out"

In Memoriam Fred Dibnah, Steeplejack and TV personality.

So. Farewell
Then Fred
Dibnah.

Famous steeplejack
From Bolton.

You climbed to
Amazing heights.

Now you are
Going up
Even higher.

E.J. Thribbnah (17½)

Also. Farewell
Then Howard
Keel.

Star of Hollywood
Musicals such as
*Seven Brides for
Seven Brothers.*

Not to be
Confused with
The Magnificent Seven
With its memorable
Theme tune.

All together
Now –

Dum Di-da-da-dum
Dum Di-da-da-dum
Da-da
Di-da-DA-da...

PPS: So. Farewell
Then
Yasser Arafat.

E.J. Thribb (17½)

In DeLorean *(shurely 'In Memoriam'? Ed)* John DeLorean, Innovative Automobile Manufacturer

So. Farewell
Then John DeLorean,
Centre of a 1980s'
Scandal involving
Taxpayers' money
And a suitcase of
Cocaine.

Your car was
Famous for having
Wings.

Have you now
Got wings?

I wonder where
Have you gone?

E.J. Thribb (17½)

DULL PLANET FOUND

'Nothing There' Say Jubilant Scientists

by Our Science Correspondent

PICTURES of what is perhaps the most boring planet in the solar system were unveiled yesterday by excited European space scientists.

The planet 'Yorn', one of the moons of 'Zirg', was revealed to be of no interest whatsoever.

The space probe has travelled billions of miles through space on a journey lasting several years in order to record just how boring the planet is.

Said one scientist, "It's amazing. There is absolutely nothing there. Look! Nothing at all. This is the most exciting discovery we have ever made."

IS THIS a giant canyon with a lake containing huge banana-eating fish who can communicate telepathically?

No.

Inside ● More pix of the galaxy's dullest planet **2, 3, 4, 5, 6, 7, 94**

"Well, I'm glad our little talk achieved something anyway"

RELATE

McLACHLAN

THE UKRAINE PRESS GAZETTE

Friday 24 December 2004

Before

After

WAS OPPOSITION LEADER POISONED?

by Our London Staff R. Senic and Di Oxin

RUMOURS are sweeping the British capital that the massively unpopular Opposition leader Mikhail Howard has been poisoned.

Nothing else, say observers, could explain the extraordinary change which has come over the Transylvanian-born party leader in the last few weeks.

"A month ago," said a close colleague, "Mikhail still seemed to be his old ineffective self. But then suddenly he became even more useless, talking total gibberish.

"Now he's making no sense at all on anything. Yesterday, for instance, he said that ID cards were a fundamental assault on liberty, and that he was all for them.

Headless Chicken Kiev

"It's the same on everything. The war. Europe. Tax. Fish. You name it – he's against it and for it in the same breath. There can only be one explanation. Someone has put something in his brown windsor soup."

Howard is known to have had dinner recently at the Beefsteak Club with members of the security services. When he returned home before dawn, his wife noticed that there was blood on his breath and that two of his teeth were protruding unnaturally.

"Something had clearly happened to Mikhail," said Mrs *(cont'd. p. 94)*

TV Highlights
What You Missed

Not only Bad, but also Unfunny (Channel 4)

STUNNINGLY revealing and accurate new bio-pic portrays the late Peter Cook as he really was – a twisted, malevolent wife beater who may well have been Jack the Ripper. Actor Dai Charmless gives an uncanny portrayal of an unpleasant and humourless man possessed by inner demons whose only desire was to murder his diminutive comic partner, the abused paraplegic Dudley Moore played by Argle McGargle. We trace Cook's life from his early days at Eton through Oxford and the great Spotlight Revue where he teamed up with David Frost and Christine Keeler for the immortal Edinburgh show "Beyond a Joke". From there it was all downhill as Cook drank, took drugs and married various women until his death thirty years later. He never produced another joke.

THE DUMB PINTER

A Play In One Act

The curtain rises on an agreeable, book-lined drawing room in Labroke Grove. An elderly playwright, Sir Harold Pinterello, is seated at his desk, writing busily. Enter Lady Magnesia, his wife, carrying a tray of tea and cakes.

Lady Magnesia: Hullo, darling, what are you writing?

(Long pause.)

Lady Magnesia: It can't be another play, since you've told everyone that you're not writing any more of those.

(Long pause.)

Lady Magnesia: Let me guess. Is it a poem?

(Long pause.)

Lady Magnesia: Or is it one of those wonderful letters to the Guardian about how Mr Bush is a fucking war criminal?

(Very long pause indeed. Curtain)

BLUNKETT RESIGNS

I'm going to spend more time with someone else's family

Daily Mail
DAVID BLUNKETT
An Apology

OVER the last few weeks, in common with all other newspapers, we may have inadvertently given the impression that we in some way believed Mr Blunkett to be unfit for high office. Headlines such as 'Blunkett's Lover's Nanny Visa Shame', 'Fast Track Your Own Resignation, Home Secretary' and 'Go Now, You Bearded Bastard' may have led readers to believe that this newspaper felt that Mr Blunkett should relinquish his post at the Home Office.

We now realise that nothing could be further from the truth and that, on the contrary, Mr Blunkett was a political colossos amongst pygmies with an extraordinary record of achievement in office, as well as huge personal courage and dedication. His departure is a tragic loss to the government, this nation and indeed the whole world.

© *The David Mail* (Surely *'The Daily Blunkett'*? Ed.)

THAT CABINET RESHUFFLE IN FULL

OUT GOES

Bearded bully. Thought to be arrogant, overbearing and short tempered.

IN COMES

Bully with beard. Thought to be short tempered, arrogant and overbearing.

BLUNKETT
The Timetable Of Events

Wednesday 3.27pm
Journalists all leave early to go Christmas shopping.

Wednesday 5.55pm
Blunkett resigns.

Wednesday 5.56pm
Editor says "Fuck!".

Wednesday 6.01pm
Journalists told to come back to office and write thousands of words on Blunkett saga.

Wednesday 6.03pm
Journalists go to bottom of barrel to find clichés.

Wednesday 7.03pm
Journalists go to barrel beneath earlier barrel.

Wednesday 7.32pm
Editor says "I know – why don't we do a Timetable of Events? They always fill up some space."

That Blunkett Resignation Speech In Full

...love ...sacrifice ...little lad ...toddler ...integrity ...decency ...little one ...honesty ...holding baby ...responsibility ...family ...care ...little boy ...my fourth and youngest ...got caught lying by my own enquiry, er ...did I mention the little boy? *(continues for several hours)*

RADIO HIGHLIGHTS

OPERA ON THREE
90.2 – 92.4FM

Berlusconi Innocenti
by Giovanni Paparazzi. Performed by the Sicilian Philharmonic Orchestra, conducted by Alessandro Capone.

Act One
The robber-baron Count Berlusconi has at last been taken into custody after years of brigandage. Wearing his trade-mark gypsy bandana, he sings the aria *Che sono tutti Communisti bastardi*, in which he cries to heaven that he has been framed by his left-wing opponents.

Act Two
The chorus of magistrates are unimpressed by the brigand-leader's plea, and sing the famous "Monopoly", chorus *Va alla prisone, ne passagero go, ne collecta due cento libra*. For our hero, all looks black (Conrad).

Act Three
In a miraculous reversal of fortune, Berlusconi is found innocent of all charges. The magistrates have discovered some important new evidence concealed in brown envelopes. They sing *Siamo Millionaire, grazie a Silvio!* Freed at last from the shadow that has hung over his life for many years, he returns in triumph to his old carefree life, robbing the poor to give to the rich (himself).

"Aren't you some bloke off the telly?"

MIDLANDS FAITH SCHOOL TOPS LEAGUE TABLES

by Our Education Staff **Ruth Jelly**

A TOP Midlands public school has been rewarded for its decision to become a Muslim faith school by topping this year's secondary school league tables.

Last year, St Cake's was 907th on the national list, coming bottom in every category.

Since changing its name to Al Qaek's, and restricting entry only to the daughters of very rich Asian businessmen, the school has seen its academic record soar.

Said the headmaster, Mr Yussef Islam (formerly Mr R.J. Kipling BA, Leicester), "We are delighted with this dramatic turnabout in our school's fortunes. As the school motto has it, *'All praise to the prophet, and death to the infidel'*".

The motto was previously *'Quis paget entrat'* ('Who pays gets in').

"Today in woodwork we're going to finish building the school"

PARENTS FIGHT TO GET INTO 'SINK SCHOOLS'

by Our Education Staff **Lunchtime O'Level**

IN RESPONSE to the government's edict to top universities insisting that they take a large proportion of children from "low achieving schools", middle-class parents are now competing for places in so-called "bog-standard comprehensives".

Typical parents Mr and Mrs Fotherington Maltby-Smythe originally had their son, Crispin, entered for Eton.

"We now realise," they said, "that he has no chance of university entrance from Eton, so we have decided to make the big sacrifice and have moved into a caravan on a travellers' site in the catchment area of the James Callaghan Comprehensive (1,758th in the league tables).

"Only this way," they continued, "can we guarantee him a really bad education and ensure that he achieves sufficiently low grades to get into a decent university."

LET'S PARLER ESPANOL
con *David Beckham*

Now you too can learn to speak fluent Spanish in only 10 seconds, with the aid of someone in the next room telling you what to say through your earpiece.

Phrase 1
¿ Donde están las prostitutas, señor?
(Translation: I am very happy to be playing for Madrid even though I have been dropped from the team.)

That's enough Spanish. Ed.

Who Are They – The 'Opus Toni'?

by Our Religious Affairs Correspondent **Cristina O'Donut**

EDUCATION Minister Ruth Kelly is only one of an ultra orthodox group of adherents to the cult of Blairism that is trying to take over Britain.

Ruthless

Opus Toni (translated as *"Everything Tony does is great"*) was founded in 1997 by the charismatic preacher Antonio Escoblair (now canonised as St Toni of Baghdad).

Disciples believe in a fanatical devotion to the leader and vow absolute obedience to whatever decision is made by the small coterie of ruthless fundamentalists who surround him.

Little Leo-nardo

The group came to light recently when it was featured in the best-selling book 'The Gordon Code' by Dan Brown, which claims that Tony Blair is a direct descendent of Jesus.

SHOCK CELEBRITY COUPLE TO SPLIT

THERE WAS widespread shock and disbelief this week, when it was announced that an extremely famous and attractive married couple were going to separate.

Front pages devoted to the Tsunami earthquake were cleared to make way for this incredible story, as few reporters could deny that the famous couple splitting up was an equally world-shattering once-in-a-lifetime event.

NOT FRIENDS

"We are completely stunned," said Hollywood commentators. "We never expected an extremely famous and attractive Hollywood couple to get bored with each other and end their marriage in this way – it's completely without precedent.

"Let's hope something like this never happens again."

Letters to the Editor

The Jerry Springer Controversy

Dear Sir,

There comes a point beyond which no decent television viewer can be pushed. And that moment came for me when I turned on BBC2 expecting to see 'Jerry Springer The Opera', a blasphemous and outrageous farrago of filth and degradation, only to find that I had tuned in at the wrong time and indeed the wrong channel, thus ending up instead watching an entirely innocuous German satellite pornography show.

I therefore had no option but to set fire to my television set before issuing a death threat to myself. May I urge other viewers to do the same?

Yours (not as disgusted as I had hoped),

SIR HERBERT GUSSET,
The Old Rectory,
Yoghurt St Ivel,
Dorset.

BRITON RELEASED FROM PRISON 'HELL ON EARTH'

by Our Political Staff **Juan Tanamo**

A BRITISH prisoner last night was allowed to walk free from what has been called "the most degrading penal institution in the western world".

Her release came after five days and nights of imprisonment, living with a gang of similarly brutalised inmates, totally cut off from any contact with the outside world.

Big Sister

Looking gaunt, strained and wild-eyed, the 65-year-old Germaine Greer told waiting newsmen, "It was worse than living under a Fascist tyranny. We were humiliated, deprived of sleep and our every move was monitored round-the-clock by TV cameras under blinding arc-lights".

Dr Greer, 76, an innocent Cambridge academic who breeds geese up the M11, was imprisoned after being suspected of wanting to earn large sums of money and to be on television.

Once locked away from the world, she was forced to dress up in mediaeval clothing and ordered to participate along with her fellow prisoners in a series of sadistic rituals organised by the camp authorities.

Germaine Warfare

After her gruelling ordeal, Dr Greer said, "I have been deeply traumatised by this experience. I had no idea that such things could go on in the so-called civilised world".

Dr Greer is said to be consulting her lawyers over the question of compensation for her horrendous experiences in captivity.

She is also receiving counselling to help her come to terms with the fact that she has made an idiot of herself.

Dr Greer is 106.

That All-Purpose Female Columnist's Attack On GERMAINE GREER

GERMAINE GREER used to be my idol. When I was a young girl, *The Female Eunuch* was my personal bible and Germaine was the feminist icon who opened my eyes and showed the whole world how a real woman could be intelligent, attractive, feisty and funny all at once – like me.

Germaine was a role model for us sisters who learned the importance of solidarity and *(Get on with attacking her or you're fired. Ed.)*

But now after her early departure from the Big Brother house, I reluctantly have to say that Germaine is a fat, old, wrinkled, washed-up, desperate, snob-bish, arrogant, hypocritical, stupid, *(This is much better. Ed.)* ugly, foolish, fat, old, fat, fat, old, fat, old, fat, fat, fat, fat *(cont. p. 94)*

AFRICA: MISSIONARY SEEKS POSITION

I gather you had to wait a long time before becoming leader too

MAN THINKS BLAIR IS 'GOOD PRIME MINISTER' SHOCK

by Our Political Staff **Phil Myglass**

THE WORLD of politics was rocked to its foundations when a Wantage man, Robert Jackson MP, said that he "greatly admired Tony Blair".

Observers are convinced that Mr Jackson spoke voluntarily and without any form of torture being applied. One theory is that he is mad *(cont. p. 94)*

SPOT THE DIFFERENCE
The IRA And Criminals

Criminals	IRA
Wear Ski Masks	Wear Ski Masks
Carry Guns	Carry Guns
Terrorise Innocent Members Of Public	Terrorise Innocent Members Of Public
Rob Banks	Rob Banks
Sometimes Get Caught	Er...

THAT EASTENDERS CHARLES KENNEDY SCRIPT IN FULL

(Man enters the Queen Vic public house)

Peggy Mitchell: I think you've had enough, Mr Kennedy. *(Ends)*

MONARCHY'S DAY OF SHAME

● EXCLUSIVE TO ALL PAPERS

by Our Entire Staff

BRITAIN's monarchy was today plunged into its worst-ever crisis, as fury mounted over the horrifying pictures that have stunned the world.

It is hard to recall a cataclysmic blunder of such proportions, which could well spell the end of the thousand-year rule of the House of Windsor.

Armageddon

Across the nation a sense of white-hot outrage swept through the entire population, as more and more voices joined the tide of protest.

Among the groups we contacted in the hope that they would be outraged were army veterans, holocaust victims and OAPs who had lived through the Blitz.

Their verdict was unanimous. "We can't see what the fuss is about," they said.

YOU DECIDE

What should be done to the Nazi prince?

Should he:

A) be forced to make a public apology from the balcony of Buckingham Palace?

B) be strung up?

C) attend counselling sessions with Dr Germaine Greer?

Daily Mail

FRIDAY, JANUARY 21, 2005

HOUSE PRICES TUMBLE AFTER HARRY OUTRAGE

By Our Harry Outrage Staff
Hans Up

PRINCE Harry's catastrophic fancy dress blunder has not only cost Britain the Olympics and stalled the Middle East peace process, it has also triggered a dramatic fall in house prices across Britain.

No, It Hasn't

From Poole to Preston, from Billericay to Bognor Regis, from Darlington to the Daily Mail, the story was the same: a house-price collapse of tsunami proportions has swept Britain.

Said one typical couple, Paul and Debby Madeupname, "Not only has Harry ruined the outcome of the Iraqi elections and hindered the eradication of world poverty, he has made

our three-bedroomed bungalow virtually worthless.

"Last week it was worth £325,000. Now our estate agent cannot give it away. Thank you, Prince Harry, for nothing."

INSIDE

Is turncoat Robert Jackson MP the biggest traitor since Judas? **94**

THICK BOY DOES SOMETHING THICK

A DIM young man did something stupid yesterday which he then regretted.

(Reuters)

TIMETABLE OF DISASTER – THE TRAGIC EVENT THAT HORRIFIED THE WORLD

6.37pm
HARRY receives phone call from Rupert saying he's going to Bingo's bash as a Zulu, which is going to be "a bloody good laugh".

6.39pm
HARRY rings Tasha who says she's going as "a Chav" and it'll be "a hoot".

6.41pm
JIGGY rings to say that she is going as a "Penguin", which will be "bloody funny".

6.43pm
PRINCE WILLIAM announces that he is going as "a lion". No one thinks this is "a scream" at all.

6.45pm
HARRY rings 'Stupid Costumes 'R Us' to find that Pongo has taken the last Ku Klux Klan outfit. "Bastard!"

6.48pm
HARRY has brainstorming session.

7.48pm
BRAINSTORMING session fails to yield results.

7.50pm
HARRY goes to costume shop to see what's left. He chooses famous "Sound of Music outfit". Tells Stiffy, "This'll be legend".

8.43pm
HARRY arrives at Bingo's dressed as Nazi. Chorus of "Boffo fancy dress, Hazza, you da man!"

8.53pm
BARFHEAD's mate, Bogbrush, takes picture of Harry on mobile phone and sends to *Sun* newspaper.

8.59pm
QUEEN abdicates, as monarchy ends.

"Me too – first sign of a daffodil and it's on with the stupid trousers and the silly shoes"

THE WEEK IN PICTURES

FANCY DRESS SHOCK

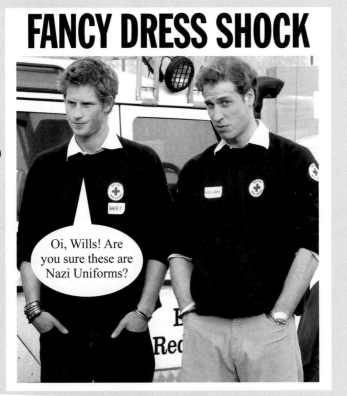

Oi, Wills! Are you sure these are Nazi Uniforms?

AN APOLOGY FROM THE PRINCE

Like I'm really sorry. Yah!

HARRY: CHARLES SPELLS IT OUT

He's got to stop mixing with these awful people

"I'm not sure having team mascots adds anything to the Games"

ME AND MY SPOON

THIS WEEK

DELIA SMITH

As the country's leading cooking expert, are there any particular spoons you would recommend?

Yes... a great big ladle full of cooking sherry, fill it right up to the brim, pour it out with a steady hand... whoops... then slug it all back.

Are spoons very important in your work?

You can shay that again! Spoons! Spoons! Teashpoons... tableshpoons... big wooden shpoons... Let's be having you! Come on, you spoons!

● Unfortunately, this week's spoon interview had to be cut short due to circumstances beyond our control. Delia Smith's new book, *Drinking For One,* is available in all good shops.

NEXT WEEK: *Anne Diamond, 'Me And My Diamond'.*

I BELIEVE THAT BRITAIN CAN ONLY TAKE A LIMITED NUMBER OF VAMPIRES EACH YEAR.

WE ARE A SMALL ISLAND. OUR BLOOD TRANSFUSION SERVICES ARE ALREADY OVERSTRETCHED AND OUR GRAVEYARDS ARE FULL TO BURSTING WITH EARTH-LINED COFFINS.

NO ONE CAN ACCUSE ME OF VAMPIRISM. I MYSELF AM A VAMPIRE AND THE DRACULAS CAME TO THIS COUNTRY FROM TRANSYLVANIA, AND WERE WELCOMED BY THE BRITISH PEOPLE WITH OPEN NECKS.

BUT NOW THE TIME HAS COME TO DEFEND OUR SHORES WITH LINES OF GARLIC AND CRUCIFIXES.

VOTE CONSERVATIVE

TOP TORY ADVISER STUNS PARTY

by Our Political Staff **Max Hustings**

A SENIOR Conservative election manager, the Australian expert Mr Bruce Blimey, stunned observers last night with a unique insight into the current political situation.

He announced to shocked campaigners that he thought the Conservative Party would not win the next election.

As seasoned party workers fainted with surprise, Mr Blimey continued, "Not only do I believe that Michael Howard will lose the next election, but my analysis also suggests that the Pope will remain a Catholic and that bears will continue to prefer woodland for the purposes of defecation".

BIRD FLU

BLOKE FLU

A Minicab Driver writes

Every week a well-known unlicensed taxi driver comments on an issue of topical importance.

THIS WEEK: **Iqbal Sacranie** (no licence-plate number or insurance etc) on the anniversary of the liberation of Auschwitz.

Blimey guv! I mean I've got nothing against the whole Holocaust business and it was you know very sad what happened but I think it's important to remember that they are not the only people we should be remembering. I mean there's the Rwandans, the Kosovans, the Kurds and the Palestinians which let's face it has got to be the worst of the lot and who's responsible for that? It's the Jews innit? No wonder they got into all that trouble. You know what I'd do with them *(cont'd. p. 94)*

(cont'd. p. 94)

THIS WEEK'S BESTSELLERS

❶ **The Da Vinci Code** by Dan Brown (1)

❷ **Decoding The Da Vinci Code** by D. Code (2)

❸ **The Da Vinci Cookbook** by D. Frost (10)

❹ **Backpackers Guide To The Da Vinci Code** (3)

❺ **The Da Vinci Code Diet** by Dee Eyett (6)

❻ **The Lovers' Guide To The Da Vinci Code** by Dr Alex Codefort (4)

❼ **The Little Book Of The Da Vinci Code** (7)

❽ **Eat, Shoots and Codes** by Dave Inchy (5)

❾ **Harry Potter And The Da Vinci Code** by Dan Rowlinginit (8)

❿ **Schott's Da Vinci Miscellany** by Dan Schott (9)

(That's enough Da Vinci books. Ed)

TORIES' FURY AT LABOUR'S SMEAR

LOOK at these two pictures. One is of Fagin, the Jewish caricature invented by the fascist Dickens to promote anti-semitism in Victorian England. The other shows the present Conservative leader as he appears in an advertisement for the Labour Party.

SEE ANY SIMILARITIES?

● **Fagin has a beard. And so doesn't Michael Howard.**

● **Fagin wears a large, black hat. And neither does Michael Howard.**

● **Fagin doesn't wear glasses. And so does Howard.**

The pictures speak for themselves. It is time to arrest Tony Blair under Mr Blunkett's Religious Hatred laws and put him in prison without trial for ever.

© All Tory Newspapers.

CONSTITUTIONAL CRISIS LOOMS

ROYAL experts say they fear that Prince Charles' marriage to the divorcee Camilla Parker Bowles may face difficulties, as it won't be accepted by certain sections of the population because "she isn't as attractive as Diana".

Said one expert, Lady Antonia Holden, "For some people, the fact that Camilla 'isn't as attractive as Diana' is a major constitutional issue that threatens to derail the chance of Charles ever being accepted as King. I think they are quite right and *(cont. p. 94)*

THOSE ALL-TIME GREAT ALASTAIR CAMPBELL ADVERTISING CAMPAIGNS

SINCE the revelation that Alastair Campbell came up with the now legendary Pigs and Shylock posters for the Labour Party, it has emerged that the former Downing Street Communications Director was also responsible for some of the other all-time classic advertising campaigns, including:

Mr Kipling makes f****ng good cakes (Mr Kipling)

Vorsprung Furch Technik (Audi)

Beanz Meanz C*ntz! (Heinz)

Hello Twats! (Wonderbra)

Guinness is good for you, you f***ing twat (Guinness)

You c**t with a Nissan (Nissan)

Go f*** yourself on an egg (The Egg Marketing Board)

Alastair Campbell isn't working (Labour Party)

ROYAL MAIL TO LOSE MONOPOLY

by Our Industrial Staff **Quentin Letters**

THE ROYAL MAIL was shocked last night at the news that it had lost its coveted monopoly.

Said a spokesman "We don't know where it's gone to. It's probably been directed to another postal service that is spelt differently, or possibly it wouldn't fit through the door and it's still in the local sorting office."

Last Post

He continued "It's always possible that an unscrupulous postal operative has stolen our monopoly. They may have seen how much money was in it and decided to take it for themselves. We just don't know for sure."

He concluded, "Our only remaining hope is that the monopoly will turn up somewhere in Britain and some kind person will redeliver it to us in one piece. It is a very valuable package and we are very upset that it has gone astray."

The Royal Mail is 198.

"I'm not crazy about these new smoking carriages"

The Sabbath Times

January 26 1943 BC

All-Day Drinking To Go Ahead

POLITICIANS have sought to play down fears expressed by some religious leaders that plans to allow 24-hour drinking in pubs and clubs in Sodom and Gomorrah will lead to a moral decline amongst the local citizens.

"All our research tells us that far from creating no-go zones, relaxing the licensing laws will actually lead to the people of Sodom and Gomorrah drinking in a more moderate and responsible way," insisted the leader of the twinned cities' council. "Wild claims that this will lead to drunken orgies in the street and vile debauchery the like of which the world has never seen before are nothing but pathetic scare stories.

"We're confident that Sodom and Gomorrah will remain the same quiet, peaceful cities after 24-hour drinking comes into force from this November."

However, local shepherd, Lot, attacked the proposals, saying, "With so much debauchery in the cities, these new measures are just rubbing salt into the wounds."

24-HOUR DRINKING

We want people to be so pissed they'll vote for us

New Oxford Entrance Examination

General Paper
(Time allowed: 3 hours)

1. Are you resident outside the United Kingdom?

2. Do you have lots of money?

3. Welcome to Oxford.

Recipe of the Day
with
Celebrity Chef
MARCO PIERRE WHITE

Battered Wife

Take one wife. Beat well.

Add police to mixture.

Pop into cell overnight to cool down.

Dish up on front pages.

Tomorrow: Fuck à l'orange.

FRIDAY, FEBRUARY 4, 2005

HAS THE DAILY MAIL BEEN INJECTED WITH BOLOX?

By **PHIL SPACE**

FRIENDS of the Daily Mail are insisting that the ageing newspaper has had a course of Bolox injections in a desperate attempt to stay looking young.

Bolox is made from a powerful poison which paralyses the brain – thus making it perfect for use in the Daily Mail.

Say friends, "The signs are all there. If you look at the piece about Princess Michael of Kent or you examine the article about Kylie Minogue it is absolutely clear that the paper is full of Bolox".

THE MAIL: Filling in with Bolox

"Now who's the fairest of them all?"

CHRIS SMITH ADMITS 'I AM LAB POSITIVE'

by Our Political Staff **Lunchtime O'Cruise**

THE FORMER Culture Secretary, Mr Chris Smith, has admitted publicly that for the past 17 years he has been "a member of the Labour Party".

Mr Smith has decided to go public to help "remove the stigma" that so often accompanies Labour membership.

He confessed to reporters, "I did not tell Tony Blair at the time that I was Labour because I thought he would disapprove. But now he has come to accept it".

Mr Blair in turn praised Mr Smith for his "courageous stance in making his condition public".

"Chris is a role model," he said, "but there is no room for his sort in my government."

Who Is Who In The Iraqi Elections

Death

POPULAR candidate with a lot of experience in the region. Would pursue a strategy of mass slaughter.

Famine

CURRENTLY an outsider but, post-election, could play a major role in Iraq's future.

War

CONTROVERSIAL figure who, if elected, can be counted on to uphold the policy of national destruction.

Plague

PROMOTING own agenda at present, but is prepared to work in an alliance with Death, War and Famine factions if necessary (*That's enough. Ed.*)

That All-Purpose Iraqi Election Leader

Day of Destiny... Moment of History... Huge turn-out... Defying terrorists... Ballots not bullets... Step forward for democracy... Day of Destiny.. Men and women patiently waiting... And still they come... Moment of History... Hard days ahead... Difficult problems to resolve... One step at a time... Harsh realities... We've no idea what's going on.

© All Newspapers.

"No, no, sir! Not that way! That way lies madness!"

CRIME SOARS TO NEW LOW

by Our Home Affairs Staff **Malcolm Mugger**

THE HOME Secretary Mr Charles Clarke last night proclaimed an astonishing breakthrough in the fight against crime.

"Since Labour came to power in 1997," he said, "we have seen crime plummeting to a record new high. This is a total vindication of Tony Blair's claim when he came to power that his government would be tough on crime and even tougher on the statistics of crime."

THOSE NEW CRIME FIGURES IN FULL

Violent crimes (*not including violence*)	**DOWN by 8%**
Violent crimes (*including violence*)	**UP by 74%**
Eating apple at wheel of vehicle	**UP by 1001%**
Alien abductions	**DOWN by 105%**
Hunting with dogs	**UP by 5,000,000%**
Binge-smoking	**DOWN by 850%**
Wearing Nazi Regalia in Public Places	**NO CHANGE – Conservative gain**

BLAIR MAKES HISTORIC APOLOGY

TONY BLAIR today made an historic public apology to the Man In The Iron Mask for his wrongful imprisonment.

"King Louis XIV of France's decision to lock up his brother Philippe in a rotting jail cell was a terrible miscarriage of justice," a clearly emotional Blair told reporters. "One that I am all too happy to apologise for – particularly during an election year."

Mr Blair thanked the Three Musketeers for their tireless efforts to clear Philippe's name, saying that but for their swashbuckling the prisoner's conviction may never have been quashed by the Court of Appeal.

BLAIR DOESN'T MAKE HISTORIC APOLOGY

TONY BLAIR today didn't make an historic public apology to those British men wrongly imprisoned in Guantamo Bay and Belmarsh Prison under anti-terror laws, who were released some years later without charge, never having beeen told what the accusations against them were.

"This was a terrible and shocking miscarriage of justice and for it my Government makes absolutely no apology whatsoever," said the Prime (cont'd. p. 94)

BORN TO BE QUEEN CONSORT

by DAME SYLVIE KRIN, author of *Born To Be Queen*, *La Dame Aux Camillas*, *Heir of Sorrows*, etc.

THE STORY SO FAR: The big day draws ever closer, but there is still much to be done.

Now read on...

ALTHOUGH the calendar said it was springtime, there was little sign of it at Highgrove.

Grey skies loured o'erhead, and a depressing drizzle obscured the outlines of Charles's new Interfaith Gazebo at the end of the yew-lined Van der Post Memorial Walk.

At a table in the Dimbley Room, Camilla was leafing disconsolately through the pile of caterers' brochures which Charles had left with her, as he had gone off by helicopter to open the new organic bus-shelter in his beloved Poundbury Village.

'Kutprice Nosh' of Reading, 'Budget Tuck' of Slough, 'All You Can Eton' of Eton. The names stared out from the glossy leaflets as if deliberately mocking her dreams.

Was this all the Royal Family was prepared to pay for, to ensure that the greatest day of Charles's life was one which no one present would ever forget?

From what she had read so far, there was precious little she could offer the 75 distinguished guests for her allocated £6.50 a head.

So far, only Wongs of Windsor had come anywhere near a wedding breakfast on the somewhat limited budget ordained by her future mother-in-law.

Camilla lit a Ross Benson and Hedges Extra-Mild Full Strength, and began reading gloomily down the bill of fare suggested by the oriental purveyors of "nuptial fare for the nobility at a price you can afford", as the proprietor Mr Wong so delicately put it in his accompanying letter.

Starter: Dim Sum
Main: Egg-Fried Rice, Chips and Beans
Sweet: Black Forest Gateau.

She groaned inwardly. How different this was going to be from what she had fondly imagined down the years... The vast banqueting hall of Buckingham Palace filled with liveried flunkeys dispensing roast swan and finest Roman Abramovich caviare to the thousands of crowned heads from all over the world.

Kings, queens, earls, grand duchesses, all drinking her health, from flutes brimming with Vintage Veuve Twankée 1983 champagne.

How cruelly all those hopes had now been dashed...

"DASHED bad news, old thing." A flustered Charles broke into Camilla's reverie, as he entered the Dimbleby Room, clutching the latest sheaf of replies to their wedding invitations.

Camilla steeled herself for what new humiliation might be heaped upon her, in addition to all those she had already had to endure.

Had the Queen decreed that she had to wear a wedding dress from the local Oxfam shop in Windsor High Street?

Would she have to leave for her honeymoon courtesy of Rashid's 24/7 Minicab Service (Heathrow only £40)?

And were her guests only allowed to throw 200 grams of biodegradable confetti-style 'Wedding Shower' under EU health and safety directives?

"Yes, Charles? What is it this time?"

She searched his face for some hint as to what might be the nature of the latest disaster to befall their supposedly 'perfect day'.

"Yes, er, well, it's about one of the family, who can't make it, after all, to our reception thingie."

Camilla's heart sank. At this rate there would soon be no one there at all.

"Who is it now?" she snapped, preparing herself for the worst.

"Actually, old girl, it's Pater. Apparently, he's discovered this long-standing commitment to... hang on, I'll read it to you."

Charles unfolded the letter, bearing the imposing crest of 'His Royal Highness the Duke of Edinburgh' over his motto 'Semper Furiens'.

Dear Prince Charles,

Thank you for inviting me to your so-called wedding on whatever day it is.

Unfortunately, looking at my diary, I see that I've just arranged to spend a few days in Germany around that time, so I shan't be with you.

Signed in his absence,
BRIGADIER RODDY HUNTLEY-PALMER
(Private Secretary to Prince Philip).

But Camilla wasn't listening.

"Your father's not coming! That's tremendous news! It's the best thing that's happened for bloody yonks!"

"Is that really how you feel, Cammers?" replied a startled Charles.

"Yes, it bloody well is," she flared, all her frustrations and disappointment over the past few months pouring out in a sudden explosion of emotion.

"Oh, that's amazing," Charles countered, warmly, "because I feel exactly the same way."

Overcome with relief, he instinctively clasped her manfully in his arms, and smiles of unbridled joy suffused both of their beaming faces.

"Oh, Chazza!"

"Oh, thingie!"

"It's going to be a wonderful day after all!"

Their lingering embrace was interrupted by a nervous cough. Sir Alan Fitztightly stood by the open door. Charles turned to face him.

"Er, can't you see I'm sort of, you know, busy?"

The Royal Equerry's face flushed with embarrassment. "I do apologise, sire," he stammered, "but it's just been on the lunchtime news."

"What has, man?" Charles snapped.

"Apparently, it is official. Mrs Parker Bowles will be Queen..."

Hearing these words was like a dream come true. Camilla was enraptured. She repeated the message again, to herself, as if in a trance. "...will be Queen ... Queen ... Queen."

Yes! Now her cup of happiness was not merely full, it positively ranneth over.

Outside, the clouds parted and a ray of brilliant spring sunshine lit up the entire landscape in a dazzling tapestry of golden light.

And was that a distant peal of church bells in the distance?

(To be continued)

Daily Mail

FRIDAY, MARCH 18, 2005

Shock NHS report

'EVERYONE IN BRITAIN WILL DIE'

By Our Pre-Election Staff
Paul Daycare

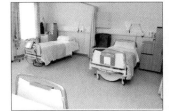

IF PRESENT trends continue, every man, woman and child alive in Britain will be dead by the year 2150. And there is nothing the NHS can do to stop this.

That is the shock finding of a top secret report compiled by senior NHS experts, which has been suppressed on Tony Blair's personal orders.

This catastrophic failure by the NHS gives the lie to government claims that Labour is looking after Britain's health better than any government before it.

As the election looms, the people of Britain have today been confronted with the stark reality that 60 million people will all be dead, the majority of them within the next 150 years.

What an indictment of Tony Blair and his policies!

Once the NHS stood for the "National Health Service" and was the envy of the world.

Today it stands only for the "National Horror Story", and means only one thing – death.

ON OTHER PAGES

■ "Vote Labour and sign your own death warrant" – Simon Heffer writes, p.10

'FOOD' FOUND IN READY MEALS – NEW SCARE

by Our Environment Staff **Sue Danwun**

CONSUMERS were warned today to check the labels of their supermarket ready meals carefully, after some were found to contain traces of food.

"This substance known as food has been linked to cancer, obesity, heart disease and flatulence," warned a food standards agency spokesman. "We can't allow dangerous substances such as food into the food chain."

However, supermarket groups tried to play down the scare, saying the amounts of food present in these meals were so tiny that they wouldn't pose any threat to health."

"Damn! I knew it was a mistake to bring these shoes!"

Who Is The Father Of Kimberly's Baby?
YOU DECIDE!

Is it:

(a) Simon Hoggart?
(b) V.S. Naipaul?
(c) Sir Trevor McDonald?
(d) Sir Max Hastings?
(e) Stephen Fry?
(f) Martin Bashir?
(g) Wayne Rooney?
(h) The Duke of Edinburgh?

Phone now on 845-2424124 and help clear up what they are calling the Mystery of the Millennium!

IDENTITY THEFT ON INCREASE

by Our Crime Staff **I.D. Card**

THERE has been a disturbing rise in the number of cases of identity theft, warned the police yesterday. Determined thieves are targeting and then impersonating innocent individuals in order to cash in on their assets.

The Tony Party

In one particularly shocking case, a Mr Howard of Transylvania found that he had all his policies stolen and the criminal wandered around Britain pretending to be him.

"It was uncanny," said Mr Howard. "I turned on the television and found this man talking about asylum, law and order, privatisation and superbugs in hospital as if he were me. It was so blatant. The only thing he hadn't stolen was my name, still calling himself Tony Blair. He must be caught before he defrauds me of the entire election."

Mr Blair is Mr Howard.

The Daily Tehranagraph

Friday March 18 2005

Schoolgirl loses fight to wear traditional dress

*by our Educational Staff **Michael Burka***

IN AN historic court ruling, the Iranian high court yesterday threw out the controversial bid by an English-born pupil for the right to wear the traditional gym-slip when attending school.

The judge listened with barely concealed impatience to evidence that in the girl's country of origin, wearing the gymslip was regarded as a very important cultural symbol.

For hundreds of years, the judge was told, female schoolchildren in the west had been expected to wear this traditional garment as a badge of uniformity and obedience to the strict code originally laid down by a sixth-century nun, St Trinian.

The judge angrily rejected all

the arguments for the plaintiff, saying that it was a fundamental human right of all schoolgirls to wear any clothing they like, so long as it was black and full-length.

(*Reuters*)

GIRL GETS DRUNK ON 19TH BIRTHDAY SHOCK

STUNNING NEWS emerged last night, when it was revealed that a girl had got drunk on her nineteenth birthday.

A source close to the girl said, "I'm truly shocked by this. The amount of times this kind of thing happens on a 19-year-old's birthday can be counted on the legs of a millipede."

Charlotte Church is 19.

"I remember you when you were this high"

THE BOOK THAT NO-ONE WANTS TO READ

EXCLUSIVE TO PRIVATE EYE

THE INSIDER DEALER

The Secret Diaries of Piers Moron

PIERS MORON is Fleet Street's Best-Known Moron. Controversial, acerbic, but most of all moronic, Moron edited the Daily Moron for nearly 2 years before being sacked for being a moron.

Moron was at the hub of British political, social and moronic life. He knew everyone, he met everyone – prime ministers, soap stars, royalty, city analysts, policemen, officials from the Department of Trade and Industry, security men giving him a plastic bag and throwing him out of the door.

Here are his sensational insider verdicts on some of the top movers and shakers in Britain with whom he rubbed shoulders during his years at the Moron:

● **Tony Blair:** *"A bit slippery".*

● **Alastair Campbell:** *"Foul-mouthed bully".*

● **Peter Mandelson:** *"Probably gay".*

● **Diana:** *"Mixed-up Royal".*

● **Gazza:** *"Drunk footballer".*

● **Jeremy Clarkson:** *"Likes cars".*

Now read Moron's incredible account of meeting Prime Minister's wife, Cherie Blair.

May 7th 1997

I AM invited round for drinks at Downing Street. Me, Piers Moron, Fleet Street's red-top rogue, going round to see the Prime Minister! Amazing! The Prime Minister is incredibly friendly. "Hello, Moron," he says. "Would you like a knighthood? Or just a beer?" We had a good laugh about this, but then his wife Cherie came in. I could tell from the first minute she fancied me rotten. The sexual chemistry was unbelievable. But she cleverly disguised her feelings for me by trying to put me down. "Are you from the Daily Moron?" she said. "Your paper is moronic, and so are you." Tony was visibly furious with her and burst out laughing to cover up her faux-pas. "You're right," he said. "He is a total moron, but we need his support."

Tomorrow: How Cherie tried to bed me and so did Diana and so did Gazza.

Reprinted from *Insider Dealer*, £19.99, The Moron Press.

The Alternative Rocky Horror Service Book

No. 94 A Service for the Fudging of the Schism

President: Dearly beloved, we are gathered here in a very real sense to say as little as possible about sincerely held differences of opinion that exist between members of our Anglican community over a matter that we do not wish to talk about.

(Here he may call upon representatives of the two parties to come forward.)

President: Do you, Bishop Onanugu, from the Church of the Holy Exorcist in Lagos, agree to be quiet for the next 3 years in the hope that the whole thing will blow over?

Bishop Onanugu: I don't.

President: And do you, Bishop Marvyn de Lumberjack from the Church of the Village People in Moosejam also agree to be quiet for the next 3 years?

Bishop de Lumberjack: I don't.

President: And will you further agree to love, honour and respect one another and your differing traditions for as long as you both shall live?

Both: No, we won't.

President: We will now give each other a sign of peace.

(The Bishops then exchange solemn blows in the sight of the congregation.)

President: We will now sing the Hymn of Thanksgiving for our deliverance from schism.

(All sing Hymn no. 94.)

HYMN

'Fight the good Fight. We both think we're right.'

DISMISSAL

The Archbishop of Canterbury *(for it is he)***:** I think that all went very well.

Bishops: Get lost, beardie!

© Nothing in Common Worship, 2005

BLOW TO MIDDLE EAST PEACE TALKS AS KEN REFUSES TO APOLOGISE

by Our Entire Staff **VERONICA TWADDLEY**

THE WORLD trembled on the brink of war today as London mayor Ken Livingstone stubbornly refused to apologise for comparing an Evening Standard reporter to a Nazi concentration camp guard.

As fury raged through the capitals of the world, from Tel Aviv to Baghdad, from Lagos to Reykjavik, the threat of global conflagration drew ever nearer.

Said one expert, "Unless Ken says sorry to the Evening Standard by tomorrow, nuclear armageddon will be unleashed."

He continued, "Ken Livingstone is trying to wipe out the human race and, even worse, his behaviour is affecting house prices in the capital – see our sister paper the Daily Mail for full details."

ON OTHER PAGES: More stuff about Red Ken 2, 3, 4, 5, 6, 7, 8, 94

BECKHAM BABY SHOCK

What with me being unfaithful and everything, how can I be sure it's yours?

AVIAN CHAPEAUX

HATS FOR BIRDS - all styles!!!

"Of course, it is a niche market. I realise that I'm never going to make a fortune"

FLEET STREET'S FISHWIFE (SURELY FISHNET? ED.)

■ HATS OFF – and dresses too – to Esther Rantzen, TV's glamorous granny!!??! She may be all of 64, but this OAP is not afraid to show what she's made of!!??!? And, blimey, don't she look great in her fishnet tights and high heels???!! No wonder all the geezers are a-droolin' and a-dribblin' at the sight of Esther a-sportin' and a-cavortin' in the altogether!!???! And no wonder the Naomis, the Kylies and the Zetas are eating their hearts out!!???! Talk about a glamour bombshell???!! You've said it, Mister!!???!

■ ESTHER RANTZEN!!!? Who does she think she is???!! A-posin' and a-poutin' like she was a Kylie or a Zeta!!??! She's old enough to be everybody's granny!!?! And no wonder her middle-aged children are burying their heads in shame at the sight of this sad old lady trying to turn the geezers on with her fishnet tights and stiletto heels!!?! 'That's Life' used to be your catchphrase 100 years ago, Esther!!??! All you're good for now is a walk-on role in One Foot In The Grave!!??! Geddit!!???!

■ *HERE HE IS!!!* Glenda's February Fellah – Cruz Beckham – Cruzy name, Cruzy guy!!!??!!

Byeeee!!!

PAXMAN 'ATTACK DOG' ROW

by Our Media Staff **Kirsty Bark**

BBC PRESENTER Jeremy Paxman was heavily criticised last night after comparing Labour Health Secretary Dr John Reid to "an attack dog".

Said a spokesman for the attack dog community, "How dare Paxman resort to this cheap stereotyping? Just because we bark a lot and occasionally bite people it doesn't mean that we are in any way similar to the Health Secretary".

The Battle of Chip on Shoulder

He continued, "This is deeply offensive and based on ignorant prejudice against attack dogs, who are a cultured and civilised breed. I, for example, have a PhD in History of Art and love opera and fine wine. Mr Paxman makes these snobbish assumptions merely because I speak with a canine accent".

The spokesdog concluded, "It's nonsense. When was the last time you saw an attack dog talking rubbish about the health service or sniffing Tony Blair's bottom?".

Mr Paxman later apologised for any offence to attack dogs. "It was a metaphor, a figure of speech," he said. "We all know that attack dogs aren't literally like Dr Reid who, of course, should be kept on a tight leash and muzzled to protect the public."

IRA EMBARRASSMENT

We've shot ourselves in the kneecap

Lookalikes

Marr   **Putin**

Sir,
    Have you noticed the sinister similarities between these two?
    I have heard that one has his roots in a subversive organisation involved in the dissemination of enemy propaganda. The other is a former head of the KGB.
    Should be warned about these double agent doubles?
    Yours,
    TOM HOYLE,

Leeds.

Bush   **Alexander**

Sir,
    Have you noticed the resemblance between Alexander The Great (as played by Colin Farrell in the latest Hollywood blockbuster) and George Dubya who plays the role of President of the USA?
    Could these two wannabe conquerors of the Near East be in some way related to one another? If so, er, perhaps it's better that we not be told.

    TARQUIN THYROID,
London, NW5.

Viking   **Forsyth**

Sir,
    This recently-published photograph of a Viking mask bears an uncanny resemblance to Bruce Forsyth, the well-known entertainer and game show host. I wonder if he might be able to claim direct descent – and, if so, Bruce's name might have originally been "Thorsyth"?
    By thunder, I think we should be told!
    Yours faithfully,
    JOHN ANDREWS,

Glasgow.

Winner   **Henry VIII**

Sir,
    I enclose a portrait of His Late Majesty King Henry VIII, scourge of popes, wives and monks, as sketched by Cornelys Matsys, and a Sunday Times photograph of Mr Michael Winner, gore-fest film director, insurance salesman and scourge of restaurateurs.
    Could they be in any way related or – even more horrifically – could one be a reincarnation of the other? I'd rather not be told.
    Yours,
    ANON,
London.

Oscar   **Blair**

Sir,
    I couldn't help but notice the disarming similarity between Oscar, the ambitious fast-talking stickleback of the new movie Shark Tale, and another slippery customer floundering in the Commons last week.
    Could they perchance be related?
    Yours faithfully,
    O.J. HINGSTON,

Via email.

McCririck   **Glazer**

Sir,
    Has anyone else noticed the strange resemblance between the betting pundit who usually gets it right, and John McCririck, the resident Channel 4 'dead cert' lunatic.
    I think we (and the United board) ought to be kept informed.
    Yours faithfully,
    NICHOLAS HILL,
Kingston Blount.

Kruger   **Richards**

Sir,
    I have been afraid to go to sleep recently after watching a Rolling Stones comeback tour video. Could this be in any way due to certain resemblances?
    JOHNNY WOOD
Via email.

Munster   **Kerry**

Sir,
    I don't know if anyone has pointed out the uncanny resemblance between cuddly, neo-Karloffian would-be ruler of the free world John Kerry and presidential candidate, the late Fred 'Herman Munster' Gwynne?
    ALAN ROBINSON,

Via email.

Cherie   **Duchess**

Sir,
    Did anybody else notice the resemblance between Cherie Blair, at the Vespers service for the Pope, and Goya's famous portrait of the Duchess of Alba?
    RICHARD WOODWARD,
London N20.

Child Catcher   **MEP**

Sir,
    It appears Mr Mandelson's new position was even more sinister than previously thought – what do they get up to in Brussels? Or perhaps he is trying to secure the King of Vulgaria a British passport?
    Yours, in fear,
    J. MATHIESON,
Via email.

Berlusconi   **Johnson**

Sir,
    Has anyone noticed the remarkable similarity between that walking advertisement for understated Italian elegance Silvio Berlusconi, and Britain's own menswear maestro, Boris Johnson? Are they by any chance related?
    Yours,
    ENA B. ANDANA.
Via email.

Jackson **Jagger**

Sir,
Your readers may be interested in the striking resemblance between Mr Michael Jackson and Ms Bianca Jagger. I wonder if, perchance, they are related?
Yours sincerely,
DR CHRIS SOLOMON,
Graveney, Kent.

Wallace **HRH**

Sir,
While reading the coverage of his opinion of BBC royal correspondent Nicholas Witchell, I couldn't help but notice the startling similarity between the heir to the throne, HRH Prince Charles, and Aardman Animations' Wallace, of Wallace and Gromit fame.
Could these bloody people be related?
JAMES THRESHER,
London SW15.

Emin **Kahlo**

Sir,
Both Tracey Emin and Frida Kahlo have exhibitions on in London at the moment. How long will it be before our Tracey cultivates her eyebrows to match those of the more famous feminist icon Ms Kahlo...?
Yours etc,
ENA B. RUSHTON,
London W1.

Julian **Anne**

Sir,
I couldn't resist sending you this photograph of Anne Milton, the Conservative candidate for Guildford. I am sure that they printed a picture of Julian Clary by mistake.
Best regards,
TONY OWEN,
Via email.

Palpatine **Christie**

Sir,
I can't help but notice the uncanny resemblance between Tony Christie and the Dark Lord of the Sith, Palpatine. Are they by any chance related? Dark forces at work would certainly seem to account for the otherwise inexplicable recent success of 'Is this the way to Amarillo'.
Regards,
IAIN COLLINS,
London E16.

Howler **Gordon**

Sir,
I was wondering if anyone has ever noticed the uncanny resemblance between our Chancellor and a Howler monkey?
Yours,
DOMINIC SYMON, age 11
Owestry, Shropshire.

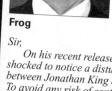

Frog **King**

Sir,
On his recent release from prison, I was shocked to notice a disturbing resemblance between Jonathan King and Kermit the Frog. To avoid any risk of confusion among your younger readers, might I urge your esteemed organ to take this opportunity to highlight the difference between the child-friendly frog and the revolting old toad?
Yours faithfully,
RICHARD CHORLEY,
Via email.

Martin **Van Gogh**

Sir,
Could it be that the late Dutch depressive and Post-Impressionist Vincent van Gogh is an ancestor of Gwyneth Paltrow's spouse Chris Martin, singer in the band Coldplay and father to young Apple?
I had always understood Van Gogh to have died childless. However, Martin is uncannily dedicated to Art and remaining unshaven.
Yours faithfully,
V. HUGHES (MRS),
London E17.

Butt-head **Letwin**

Sir,
Watching his televised response to the budget, we were struck by the startling resemblance between Oliver Letwin and Butt-head of Beavis and Butt-head. Are they by any chance related? We think we should huh-huh huh-huh be told.
HEATHER AND STEVEN CURTIS,
Coventry

Oyl **Rice**

Sir,
Have you noticed the resemblance between Condoleezza Rice and Olive Oyl? They are both attracted to men who don't realise their own strength!
PETER SCOTT,
Great Bromley, Colchester.

Kelly **Doherty**

Sir,
I wondered if your readers have noticed the resemblance between Education Secretary Ruth Kelly and tormented musician Pete Doherty, each of whom has ended up mixing with an unsavoury crowd.
Yours faithfully,
MATT LEWIS,
London SW17.

Genghis **Galloway**

Sir,
I wonder if anyone has noticed the similarity between "an outcast who created the biggest land empire the world has ever seen", General Galloway, and that very Respectful warlord Genghis Khan.
With Respect,
R. BENT,
Edinburgh.

IRA – NEW SHOCK

We believe in law and order – and we'll shoot anyone who says we don't

"THE SASH MY FATHER WORE..."

Moron Defends 'Fake' Diaries

by Our Media Staff **Hugh Very-Ropey** and **Maddy Tupp**

FORMER Moron editor Piers Moron today defended his decision to print diaries that have now been shown to be fakes.

Experts have pointed to passages in the diaries which cannot be genuine, and which refer to events which cannot possibly have taken place. For instance:

● In his entry for June 12 1997, Moron claims to have had lunch with Elvis Presley and Marilyn Monroe at the Ivy to discuss the Iraq War.

● On March 6 2001, Moron describes watching W.G. Grace hit a century before lunch at Edgbaston.

● On May 23 1995, Moron claims that he did not know he had bought shares which had been tipped in his own newspaper.

Yesterday Moron admitted that his diaries might be fakes, but he defended his decision to publish them: "Okay, so they are not real, but they are a recreation of the sort of thing which might have happened if I hadn't made it all up".

Nursery Times

························· Friday, 4 March, 2005 ·························

'DON'T ASK ME ABOUT HUGH GRUNT!' Jemima's Plea

by Our Court Staff
Hans Moslem Andersen

LOVELY JEMIMA Puddleduck, the daughter of billionaire shark Sir Jams Goldfish, today told the Nursery Times, "I am happy to talk about my charity work, but I am not prepared to discuss my private life."

In recent weeks, Jemima's name has been linked to pig about town Hugh Grunt after the collapse of her long-standing union with Mr Imran Fox.

But this topic is out of bounds, as Jemima makes clear. "I do a lot of work for disadvantaged ducklings," she told me. "They are so sweet and it is a crime that they get eaten by people like Mr Fox."

'THE LOVE OF MY LIFE'
Blunkett tells all

by **Mary-Ann Suckup**

TODAY (and indeed every other day) the former Home Secretary reveals the innermost secrets of his heart to whichever journalist he happens to run into (or indeed ring up).

"Firstly, I would like to thank everyone in the world for being so wonderfully supportive in my recent terrible ordeal.

"I have had literally millions of letters, cards, and emails, all of them telling me how marvellous I am, and what a raw deal I have had at the hands of the media, and indeed everyone else."

I met the former Home Secretary in his £8 million grace-and-favour Belgravia mansion, where he tells me he is guarded round-the-clock by an elite unit of SAS bodyguards against possible assassination attempts by Osama bin Laden or Kimberly Quinn.

benefit of our photographer.

Blunkett coverage

But tears well up in David's eyes, when the conversation turns to what he calls, frankly, "the love of my life". He is still grieving at their separation, trying to come to terms with the fact that they are no longer together.

"We used to talk to each other many times a day," he says wistfully. "We were absolutely made for each other, Tony and I.

"But now, every day, when I wake up in the morning, I feel sick to the pit of my stomach at the thought that I am not going to see him.

"I just can't believe it's over." As he said this, David brought out an onion and sobbed openly for the

Wrong side of the Blunkett

"During those years we were together we gave birth to beautiful policies. But now Tony pretends to the world that they are not mine. It's very hurtful.

"He always used to say that he couldn't live without me. And yet now I have to fight every inch of the way to get access to all the things in this world I hold most dear – power, influence, the chance to appear on the *Today* programme and my right to return to the Cabinet after the election."

Security Blunkett

At this point, David's voice fades away into silence, as his assistant appears to tell me, "You've had your ten minutes. It's time for *Woman's Own* now, Mr Blunkett".

His parting words as I left the room were heartfelt. "I wish the media would leave me alone."

NEXT WEEK: Blunkett tells us more about "The greatest love of my life – myself".

© *Mills and Boon 2005.*

50

KILROY-SILK IN NEW IMMIGRATION ROW

*by Our Political Staff **Verity Arse***

THE controversial former television presenter Robert Kilroy-Silk was plunged into fresh controversy last night when he became the focus of accusations of racism.

According to eyewitness reports, millions of people in Britain believe that Kilroy-Silk "should not be allowed in Britain" and "should be sent home to Portugal where he belongs."

Said one typical member of the public, "Don't get me wrong. I'm not racist. I just don't like people who are orange."

Mr Kilroy-Silk complained bitterly about his treatment in Britain. "How dare people object to me purely because of the colour of my skin? They should object to me because of my stupid and offensive views."

Late News

■ Kilroy-Silk wins Orange Prize

What Should Camilla Be Known As After Charles Becomes King?
YOU DECIDE!

❑ The Queen
❑ Princess Consort
❑ Lady Diana
❑ Princess Fiona from *Shrek*
❑ The Artist formerly known as Camilla
❑ Ellen MacArthur
❑ Piers Morganatic

(That's enough titles. Ed.)

☎ **Phone Buckingham Palace now on 0897 345 2345**

BORIS JOHNSON

Don't believe a word of this!

CRIPES! So the boffins are telling us that mobiles are dangerous! Especially for tiny tots, whose brains they say can be turned to jelly and custard!

What rot! I use a mobile all the time, especially when I'm on my bike, ringing up my mistress and asking her what time I should come round!

And I can tell you this – there's nothing wrong with my brain! It's us grod is any bong's selses!

© Beano Boris, the *Daily Telegraph*

Join the Great Mobile Debate! Ring or text us on your mobile and c f ur branes fried!

ONCE again, half-term has been ruined by the dreaded school project! Toddler Charlie is supposed to be having some much-needed time off after a hectic first half of term at St Tweazles School For Gifted Children With Learning Difficulties! And what do they do? Give him a project which involves building a robot! In a week? Pu-lease!!

How on earth do they expect busy working mothers (some of whom have columns to write about the hell of half-term for their forthcoming collection *'We're In The Mummy!'*, Johnson & Pearson, £17.95!!) to drop everything and spend a week finding toilet rolls and tissue boxes and turning them into lovingly modelled robots?!!

It's ok for the stay-at-home mums with their part-time Art degrees and their little jobs helping out in the charity shop and their big ideas about starting up an on-line baby clothes business which are never going to happen. (No offence, but you know I'm right, girls!!) *They've* got all the time in the world to get out the sellotape and turn out something marvellous, ie cheat on behalf of their lazy offspring.

And it's alright too for the lucky children who don't have useless dads who spend the entire half-term watching Channel Four's 100 Best Celebrity Autopsies with Dr Gutner Von Haas and Jimmy Carr!! (No names, Useless Simon, but you know who you are!!)

ROLLO's dad, for example, is an architect and, would you believe it, Rollo turned up at school with a perfectly crafted model of R2-D2 from Star Wars with swivelling head and moveable feet!

Impressive! But did little Rollo build this all on his own? I think not.

No! In the Filler household we've made an ethical decision. Charlie's parents are *not* going to do his school project for him.

The au-pair is. And, luckily, Elska has a degree in Animatronics from the Ukraine's Instituta Tecknologika and has helped Charlie to construct a fully-automated warrior droid with a laser-missile-guidance system – which, incidentally, blew up Rollo's pathetic apology for a robot along with most of the art room!!! A+ for Charlie, I think, Miss Jarvis!!

© P. Filler.

Is This The Beast Of Wood Lane?

RESIDENTS of White City have been warned to be on their guard, following several sightings of what one terrified man described as "the director-general of the BBC".

He is already believed to have struck once, savaging an innocent television journalist in an unprovoked assault which left its victim traumatised.

"I was frightened for my life," he told the Eye. "I sold up and went to live in Rwanda. It's much safer there."

All inhabitants of the White City area have been advised to lock their doors at night and to keep away from the BBC TV Centre where the beast is believed to have his lair.

Savage Cuts

The RSPCA advised the public "not to approach Mark Thompson under any circumstances and to have a precautionary tetanus injection just in case".

If you think you have seen the beast, contact Jeremy Paxman on paxocomeoffit@bbc.co.uk

Easter Treat for All the Family!

OLIVER!

The classic musical about the little boy who complains about school food and asks "Please sir, can I have some more money?"

Who can forget the tyrannous Mr Blair's outraged response "More? Can't we set up a Food Trust and get OFSTED to look into the issue instead?"

Includes all your favourite songs.

★ *Food, Disgusting Food*

★ *Who Will Fry?* ♪

♪ ★ *I'd Eat Anything*

★ *Consider Yourself... At Risk*

★ *You've Got to Eat a Nugget or Two!*

★ *I'm Reviewing the Whole School Dinner Situation*

Cast in Full

Jamie Oliver	Jude Law
Mr Bumble	Tony Blair
The Artful Dodger	Ruth Kelly
Bill Sykes	Charles Clarke
Fagin	Margaret Hodge

THAT MISSING PARAGRAPH IN FULL

PRIVATE EYE can exclusively reveal the explosive censored paragraph in Mrs Wilmshurst's sensational resignation letter that once again questions the legality of the invasion of Iraq:

I have decided to resign, as I can no longer tolerate the ▇▇▇ of this government which has consistently ▇▇▇ed, ▇▇▇ed, and ▇▇▇ed again through their teeth.

The Attorney General, Lord Goldsmith, is ▇▇▇ a man of integrity. On the contrary, he has shown he is ▇▇▇ capable of telling the truth.

In fact, his pants are on ----.

As for the Prime Minister, Mr Tony ▇▇▇, I have ▇▇▇ respect for him. He just does whatever President ▇▇▇ tells him.

LAST NIGHT, the government defended the censored passages, saying that legal advice was confidential, especially when it made the Attorney General look like a total ▇▇▇er.

Nursery Times

Friday, 13 March, 2005

NEVERLAND TRIAL

Day 94

by Our Crime Correspondent
Captain Crook

IN THE most bizarre case ever to hit the world of nursery stories, Mr Peter Pan today took the stand in his pyjamas to answer charges of "Corrupting Lost Boys".

The accusations come from a Michael Darling who was befriended by Mr Pan and then taken to the fantasy world of Neverland.

Mr Pan's lawyers claim that the accusations are merely attempted blackmail and that the child was being put up to it by his mother, Mrs Darling.

The child claimed that Mr Pan had got him "high", flying through the sky to the third star on the right and straight on till morning, and had then shown him and his brother images of mermaids and Indian princesses.

Said Mr Jackson, "I deny all these alligators."

On Other Pages
● Why can't Humpty Dumpty be put back together again? NHS scandal. p2 ● Goldilocks sells burglary story to BBC. p3 ● Wolf in Grannie ID theft. p94

Let's Parler EU!

(as told to Kilometres Kington de *La Independent*)

Numero 94: Le Diplomacy

Monsieur Blair: Ah, Monsieur Chirac! Je suis un tremendous supporter de vous et votre constitution non-Federale!

Monsieur Chirac *(pour c'est lui)*: Soddez-vous off, matey! Vous êtes un creep anglais qui supports Bush – un vrai lunatique.

Monsieur Blair: Un peu harsh, surement, Jacques?

Monsieur Chirac: Pas du tout! Et while nous sommes about it, nous ne vous donnerons pas votre three billion pounds back!

Monsieur Blair: Mais c'est unfair! Nous sommes amis, n'est-ce pas?

Monsieur Chirac: Je suis in a tremendous rebate! Geddez-vous it? C'est un joke! C'est le famous sense of humour anglais!!

Monsieur Blair: Boo hoo hoo!

Monsieur Chirac: Ha ha ha!

(To be continued)

- PILBROW -

"Jamie Oliver made me change it"

CHRISTMAS PETS: A GUIDE TO LONGEVITY

DOG	CAT
"FOR LIFE"	"FOR LIFE"
TORTOISE	MAYFLY
"FOR SEVERAL LIVES"	"JUST FOR CHRISTMAS"

COMBINED BESTSELLERS: 'THE DA VINCI HIGHWAY CODE'

SHOCK MURDER AT START — ENTER OUR HERO... — EXAMINES CRIME SCENE — ACQUIRES SEXY ASSISTANT

THEY TRAVEL WIDELY — 'LAST SUPPER' IS ANALYSED — REVEALS JESUS NOT DIVINE... — HE FATHERED A CHILD

KNIGHTS TEMPLAR IMPLICATED... — ...AND THE VATICAN... — HOLY GRAIL IS LOCATED. — NOW BUY THE SEQUEL

JACKO: THE RETITLED RE-RELEASES

OFF THE HOOK — UN-INDICTABLE

NOT BAD AFTER ALL... — LEGal HIStory — PAST, PRESENT, NO FUTURE

AND NOT DANGEROUS EITHER!... — Fibber?

TOWELS: THE COMPLETE GRAMMAR

His — Hers — Mine

Theirs — Ours...all ours!

CLARKSON: THE FINAL ROAD TESTS

VERY POOR BRAKING... — TERRIBLE RIDE POSITION...

ZERO SUSPENSION... — TOP SPEED 30 MPH... NO ACCELERATION... ONLY IN BLACK...

DEIDRE'S NURSERY RHYME CASEBOOK: THE OWL

OWL HAS A NEW LODGER... — Sorry, I thought I was alone... — It's OK — Pussy — Wow! She's gorgeous!

HE FALLS IN LOVE... — Sigh!

ONE BOOZY NIGHT: — oh ~ owl! oh ~ Cat!

BUT... — I'm late... — oh no! What now?

DEIDRE SAYS ~ Interspecies love is wrong. Leave the country, marry abroad. P.S. Take some honey and plenty of money.

ROVER: HIS FINAL TRICKS

Thanks, Phil M.

Brum News CHINESE FLOWN IN FOR TALKS — FETCH

Brum News PLEA FOR GOVT. AID — BEG

Brum News TALKS FAIL ROVER TO CLOSE — ROLE OVER

P45 — PLAY DEAD

MOLEHILL INTO MOUNTAIN: HOW IT HAPPENS

MOLE BUILDS ILLEGAL STRUCTURE — REFUSED × APPLIES FOR RETROSPECTIVE PERMISSION — GRANTED ✓ APPEALS AS OPPRESSED MINORITY — GETS AID FROM E.U. MOLE-REHOUSING FUND

SUBMITS NEW PLANS FOR APPROVAL — REBUILT TO INCORPORATE SOCIAL HOUSING, DISABLED MOLE ACCESS, INSULATION, FIRE DOORS, CYCLEWAY, ETC. — END RESULT

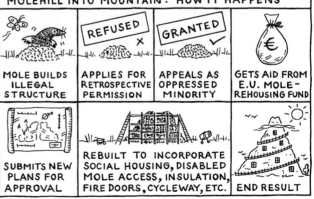

THOSE BIG ELECTION ISSUES IN FULL

① **Abortion**
② **Gypsies**
③ **School dinners**
④ **Whatever else is in the Daily Mail today**
⑤ **Er...**
⑥ **That's it.**

© New Labour/Conservative

NEW WORDS

Traveller (noun)   Person who doesn't go anywhere

Mobile home (noun)   House that is permanently fixed in one location

Campsite (noun)   Executive Housing Development

Gypsy (noun)   Citizen who wishes to reside in a settled community safe from the threat of being uprooted and forced to move elsewhere at irregular intervals

(That's enough new words. Ed)

DO YOU SUFFER FROM IRRITABLE JOWELL SYNDROME?

Millions of people experience the trauma of IJS whenever they see Tessa Jowell on television or read about her in the newspapers.

Symptoms include: ● **nausea** ● **heartburn** ● **uncontrollable rage** ● **homicidal urges**.

If you are a victim of IJS, there is no known cure and you just have to learn to live with it.

Issued by the IJS Society of Great Britain

"He's very good – he never complains when I can't afford things for him"

ABORTION LATEST

I'm fighting for the rights of the undead

Surely "unborn", Michael?

"Daleks! Form a circle!"

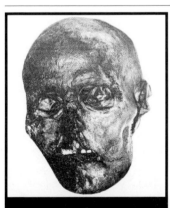

Before

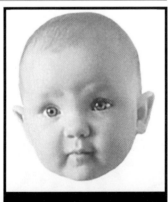

After

Has Michael Douglas had plastic surgery?

by Our Showbiz Staff **Hugh Cares**

HOLLYWOOD experts are convinced that the ageing star of Fatal Attraction has had a nip-and-tuck to try and turn back the biological clock.

PR men for the movie legend say it's all down to improved diet and a new exercise regime, but close observers say that Michael's new youthful look would be impossible without surgical procedures.

But the star himself remained tight-lipped because his face doesn't move any more *(That's enough of this rubbish. Ed.)*

GLENDA SLAGG

FLEET STREET'S TURKEY TWIZZLER!!

■ SO POOR old Becks wants his nippers to be left alone?!! Gawd Almighty?!?! Then why not give them sensible names like Glen or Glenda and stop parading them in front of the paparazzi every time your marriage is on the rocks – i.e. all the time?!?!? Geddit?! Do us a favour, David – why don't *you* leave *us* alone?! Geddit?!!

■ SHED A TEAR for poor little Romeo, Brooklyn and the other one *("Cruz" – Sub-Ed)*??!?! Why can't the evil paparazzi respect the rights of these little 'uns to a bit of privacy in their lives like anyone else!?! Hang on a minute?! What am I doing writing about them? I should be ashamed of myself. In fact, I'm going to stop *right* now!?!?!

Byeeee!!!
(Come back or you're fired. Ed.)

■ SO PRINCESS Beatrice is dyslexic?!? And proud of it! Pull the other one, Fergie?!! Your kid's a thicko – just like her Mum 'n' Dad!?! No offence, Ma'am!?! But I guess it runs in the family. It's the stoopid gene?!? I saw a programme all about it on the telly!?!

Byeeee!!!
(Come back – you haven't done your 'hats off to Fergie' bit yet. Ed.)

■ HATS OFF to Fergie!?! She and brave Princess Beatrice have given hope to millions of mums and daughters who struggle with the problems of dyslexia!?!? Good on yer, Ma'am – you're a shining example to us all!?!? You may find it hard to believe this but I myself can barely read or write (especially after lunch) and yet I have managed to overcome my handicap and become Fleet Street's Feature Writer of the Year in the 2005 UK Press Awards!?!?!?

Byeeee!!!
(No. Come back – you haven't done the 'Bonk Holiday Hunks' yet. Ed.)

HERE THEY ARE – Glenda's Bonk Holiday Hunks:

● **Paul Wolfowitz** – He's running the World Bonk!?! You can put a deposit in my security box any day, Wolfie!?!!?

● **Mark Thompson** – the BBC's top dog! Geddit?!? You can sink your teeth into this gal any day, Wolfie!?!?

● **James Dyson** – Mr Vacuum Cleaner, stoopid!?! You say you don't need a bag anymore – what? Not even li'l ol' me???! Geddit?!!

Byeeee!!!
(All right. You really are fired. Ed.)

Zimbabwe Telegraph
FRIDAY APRIL 15 2005

BRITISH ELECTION RIGGED
Mugabe Lashes Blair

by Our Man In London **Lunchtime O'Noose**

ZIMBABWEAN observers were last night expressing their fears that the British general election will be invalid, thanks to widespread vote-rigging and fraud by the leader of the ruling Labour Party, the power-crazed Tony Mugablair.

Already, evidence is mounting from all over the country that Mugablair's henchmen in such remote settlements as Birmingham are forging huge quantities of postal votes in order to deliver an overwhelming Zanulabour victory.

One of the few independent judges left in Britain with the courage to speak his mind yesterday compared his country's corrupt voting system to that of a 'banana republic'.

Our beloved leader President Mugabe was rightly outraged by the horrifying news of how Britain's election was being stolen by its hated dictator. "Mugablair," he said, "has shocked the civilised world. He should step down at once and allow the real winner of the election to take over as rightful leader of the British empire, ie myself."

The sort of headlines that fuel Charles's anti-press fury

GOD BLESS YOUR ROYAL HIGHNESS AND YOUR BEAUTIFUL DUCHESS

THREE CHEERS FOR HAPPY COUPLE ON GLORIOUS DAY

TOGETHER AT LAST! HAPPY END TO EPIC LOVE STORY THAT SPANNED DECADES

FOR GOD'S SAKE, MAKE CHARLES KING NOW!

(That's enough lack of respect. Ed.)

Everyone's calling me self-pitying. It's so unfair

THE CAMILLA I HAVE NEVER MET

by Her Best Friend Lady Annabel Strypt-Pyne

THOSE of us who know Camilla know that she is a down-to-earth, good-hearted country woman who likes nothing better than to put her green-wellied feet up on her dog and indulge in a cigarette and a big glass of gin and tonic.

She is a long way from the public image of a woman who lives in the country, wears green wellies and likes a drink and a smoke.

No, the real Camilla is *(That's enough. Ed.)*

CHITTY CHITTY BANG! BANG! BANG! BANG!

ROBERT THOMPSON

"My, how children have changed over the years!"

GREATEST MAN IN HISTORY OF WORLD DIES

MILLIONS OF TRIBUTES FLOOD IN
"AND STILL THEY COME..."

by **Our Entire Staff**

TODAY I watched with my own eyes as Sky TV showed us how the Eternal City has become a living river of pilgrims, all with only one thought in their minds – "Where's the toilet?" *(Surely, "We must pay our last respects to the greatest pope since St Peter"? Ed.)*

And still they came, from every corner of the globe and from all walks of life – young and old, rich and poor, black and white, gay and straight.

I saw nuns weeping on the shoulders of gnarled Samurai warriors.

Zulu tribesmen embraced Inuit grandmothers. Aztec priests solemnly conducted sacrifical rituals as a tribute to the man they knew simply as "El Cid". *(Can this be right? Ed.)*

And still they came. A human tide that stretched from the Tiber to Trieste.

And still my article flowed on, like a living river of drivel, filled with words of every shape and form – long and short, large and small, native and foreign – all mingled together in one mighty cornucopia of grief *(continued pages 2, 3, 4, 5, 6, 7, 8, 94)*
© *All newspapers.*

Who Will Be The New Pope?

As the world's top cardinals huddle together behind locked doors, who are the hot tips for the man who will be the new "Top of the Popes"?

Joseph Ratpoison, 79, Archbishop of Warfarino. A noted hardline liberal, with profoundly conservative views on issues ranging from abortion to women priests, Ratpoison is a noted linguist, speaking 17 languages, including Croatian, Walloon and Klingon.

Ignatius Onanugo, 69, Archbishop of Rumbabwe. A liberal hardliner, with traditionalist views on issues ranging from abortion to women priests, Onanugu is hotly tipped to be the first black pope since Pope Othello I in the 4th Century BC.

Jesus-Maria Guevara, 83, Bishop of Santa Assassinato. A former revolutionary, who embraced liberation theology in the 1960s, Guevara is now an entrenched Conservative who opposes abortion and women priests. Guevara is hotly tipped to be the first Mexican pope since Gonzales I ('The Speedy') in the 16th Century.

P.D. O'Phile, 75, Archbishop of New Dworkin. An outspoken liberal, who embraced a number of choirboys in his diocese, O'Phile is currently serving 27 years in the New Dworkin penitentiary and is completing a PhD thesis on the life of the Blessed Michael of Jackson.

DAVE SPART (Co-Chair of the Respect Anti-War, Blair and Foxhunting Support Group, Bethnal Green) on the death of the late Pope John-Paul II.

Er... the sickening spectacle of the mass media filling thousands of pages with sycophantic tributes to the late Pope, claiming that he was somehow a champion of freedom, when he was in fact nothing less than a fascist autocrat and mass-murderer who was personally responsible for the deaths of millions of Aids victims throughout Africa and the Third World, not to mention a hardline homophobe who refused to allow gays and lesbians their freedom to marry in Catholic churches, er, how could he claim to be a 'friend of the poor' as the capitalist media have hypocritically pretended when he lived a life of luxury in huge palaces surrounded by paintings worth billions of pounds which could have been sold to raise money for the Aids victims he had killed, er, not to mention his lifelong hatred of women as was shown by his refusal to allow women to become popes, er, plus also his reactionary attempt to denigrate progressive left-wing regimes, such as Poland, the Soviet Union, Kosovo etc must mark him down as the arch-fascist of all time – on a par with, dare one say it, Adolf Hitler and Michael Howard.

You can read more of Dave Spart's forthright comments on the late Pope in the *New Spartsman*, the *Grauniad*, the *Indescribably Sparty*, and on his personal website www.spart-er-er.co.uk.

BUSH LEADS MOURNING

CANCEL THE DEBT

Make Poverty History!

Many people in the first world are being crippled by the huge amount of interest that they have to pay on money that they have borrowed. Take the sad case of Rosie, an ex-BBC broadcaster in England, who is struggling desperately to pay off the vast debts which – through no fault of anyone else – she has run up on various credit cards. Her life has been ruined by the unscrupulous western money lenders who are now trying to make her pay them back. Please join us in signing a petititon to let poor Rosie off her debts and allow her to keep her large London house, her two buy-to-let flats, her "super-chic" Paris apartment and her range of badly fitting off-the-shoulder dresses. Thank you.

....

I think Rosie Millard should have her debt cancelled. I am over 18 and completely mad.
Signed..

FAMOUS WRISTBANDS

Karl Marx's Make Property History Campaign

That Farewell 'Breakfast With Frost' Menu in full

Choice of Frosties or Cheerios

– ✳ –

Old Ham, Fried Brains and Scrambled Ego
or
Poached Gags with Wafffles, Syrup and Old Chestnuts Purée

– ✳ –

*All washed up with
Vintage Champagne in the Arse*

– ✳ –

All supplied direct from the Gaga oven

ME AND MY SPOON

THIS WEEK

SIR BOB GELDOF

Do spoons play a significant role in your life?

You should be fokkin' ashamed of yourself, talking about fokkin' spoons when millions of people are fokkin' dying in Africa. What's your paper doing about it, that's what I'd like to fokkin' know...

Can I ask you next then if you have a favourite spoon?

What's the fokkin' point of a spoon if you've got no fokkin' food? Have you ever stopped to consider that, you eejit? Jaysus, you people are thick!

Has anything amusing ever happened to you in connection with a spoon?

Oh fok it! What am I doing here answering questions about fokkin' spoons? I'm fokkin' off...

Unfortunately the spoon interview had to be cut short at this point due to circumstances beyond our control.

NEXT WEEK: *Camilla Parker-Bowles "Me And My Parker and My Bowls".*

ADAMS NEW SHOCK!

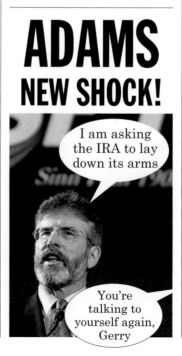

I am asking the IRA to lay down its arms

You're talking to yourself again, Gerry

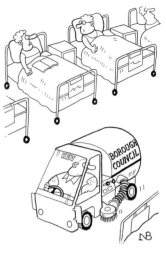

"The cleaning in this hospital isn't all it might be"

Lines On The Marriage Of Charles, Prince of Wales, to Mrs Camilla Parker Bowles

by the Poet Laureate, Andrew Motion.

I took your news
Into my garden space
(Which is basically a garden
But sounds more poetic)
To think what I could
Say in a poem.

Because that is my job.
I have to write poems on
These occasions.

So, as I said,
I took your news
Into my garden space.

The flowers are blossoming
Like your romance.
There are new shoots
Growing below
The dirty laundry line
Of scandal.

That's a metaphor, you see –
Green shoots are like
Blossoming flowers.
They signify a new
Beginning.

A new beginning. Yes.
That's what the poem needs.
And probably a new end.

But, apart from that, I
Think it's quite good.

© *Andrew GoingThroughTheMotions*

BORN TO BE QUEEN CONSORT

by DAME SYLVIE KRIN, author of *Born To Be Queen, La Dame Aux Camillas, Heir of Sorrows*, etc.

THE STORY SO FAR: After months of turmoil and confusion, Camilla and Charles have finally tied the knot and are honeymooning in the ancient palace of Balmoral.

Now read on...

"HAPPY, darling?" Charles placed an arm tenderly around his new bride's shoulders as they gazed out together over the moonlit waters of Loch Loonie and the distant snow-capped peaks of Ben Elton.

"Bloody happy, Chazza!"

Camilla drew deeply on her first full-strength Senior Citizen untipped cigarette since breakfast, and watched a garland of smoke curling up towards the ceiling of the Prince Albert Room, with its massive teak four-poster bed in the shape of a battleship – a present to Queen Victoria from her cousin, the Grand-Duke Michael of Holsten-Carlsberg.

Camilla shivered slightly in the chill Highland air and pulled the lilac satin peignoir (a wedding gift purchased at the Henley-on-Thames branch of "Knickers 'R Us" by Sir John and Lady Mortimer) closer round her ivory shoulders.

Could it really be true, the moment she had dreamed of since she was a young woman snatching the fruits of forbidden love behind the strawberry tent at one of Lord Cowpat's legendary polo tournaments?

So often in the past few frantic weeks, it had seemed as if this moment would never come.

Everything had conspired against the wedding she had longed for.

The mix-up over the service in St George's Chapel, when it had been discovered by some beastly lawyer that it would be a criminal offence for them to get married there.

All the stupid speculation in the newspapers as to whether she would be called 'Queen' or just plain 'Duchess of Windsor'.

And then, of course, there was the untimely death of His Holiness the Pope, who had chosen just the wrong moment to pass away...

No wonder Charles had lost his temper on the ski-slopes when some impertinent little journalist from the BBC had asked him whether he was looking forward to his wedding.

But in the end, somehow, it had all worked out. It had, after all, been the wedding of her dreams.

The threatened snow had failed to materialise, and instead a brilliant April sun had shone on the cheering crowd lining the streets as they did their Saturday shopping. "Come on Hedgehunter!" the people had cheered as the Rolls-Royce Phantom X waited

behind the Tesco lorry at the traffic lights leading to the register office.

And then there was the civil ceremony, the service, the reception – it all went by in a blur of happy snapshots.

The sweet, smiling archbishop with the silver beard joining them as one... the Queen kindly reminding her not to smoke in the Royal Chapel because they had already had one fire there... the young Princes up to their usual pranks pretending to be drunk and tying old boots to the train of her wedding dress... and all those people she had seen on the television. Was that really Mr Bean in a top hat...? And the gallant Sir Stephen Fry, telling everyone how "handsome" she was...? And even Charles's friend Tara Rara-Boomday had put on some clothes for a change... Yes! What a day! It would be forever embedded in the photograph album of her mind.

And now here, secluded from the world in this romantic fairy-tale castle, they could at last be man and wife in the full sense of the word...

THERE was a discreet knock at the door. It was Auld Angus McVittie, the ancient retainer. He was carrying a huge silver dish, bearing twelve dozen oysters.

"Your late great-grandfather Edward VII always swore by them when he entertained his married ladies up from London," he announced as he placed them on a table by the bed.

Charles blushed. "That will be all, McVittie," he hastily admonished the departing retainer.

As the door closed, there was a strange wailing sound from the terrace beneath the window.

The newly-weds peered down through the darkness to where, far below, a lone piper from one of Charles's beloved regiments, the 49th Highland Buffoons, was warming up to play a selection of hits from *South Pacific*.

"Listen, darling!" Charles exclaimed. "He's playing our tune!"

And so he was. The plangent strains of *Some Enchanted Evening* floated up through the night, just as they had done for every royal honeymoon couple since time immemorial.

As this romantic serenade died away on the night air, Charles moved expectantly towards the bed, where Auld Angus had laid out the tartan pyjamas he always wore when north of the border.

Camilla stubbed out her cigarette and turned down the lights. They were alone at last, just the two of them in the silence.

"Oh, Chazza!" she whispered.

"Oh, Cammers!" he breathed.

"Oh, excuse me, Your Royal Highness." A familiar voice broke in on their intimacy, as the red-headed figure of Nicholas Witchell emerged from underneath the bed.

"How are you enjoying your honeymoon, sir?" asked the BBC's royal correspondent in his silkiest tones.

So this was what her new life was to be like, thought Camilla, her heart sinking like a stone.

Outside, the stars in the velvet heaven seemed to go out one by one, as the dark snowclouds gathered down the vasty sides of Glen Morangie.

(To be continued)

The Today Programme
6am

Jim Naughtie *(for it is he)*: And with the time at 6.00, this is the Today Programme, with me, Jim Naughtie, in the studio...

Caroline Quin *(for it is she)*: ...and me, Sarah Montague, on the battlebus at the Charles Clore Shopping Centre, Milton Keynes.

Naughtie: And our headlines this morning are that Tony Blair will today be announcing his new targets for nutrition standards in Britain's pre-primary school sector. Michael Howard's chosen theme for the day will be the need to get more police back into old people's homes. And Charles Kennedy will be north of the border, focussing on the underfunding of traditional rural skills programmes.

But first the news, read by Charlotte Greenpeace.

Greenpeace: The Prime Minister will today be visiting Hemel Hempstead to announce new targets for the Government's traditional rural skills programme.

The Conservative leader Michael Howard will be outlining his party's plans for better nutrition in Britain's pre-primary schools.

And the Liberal Democrat leader Charles Kennedy will be focussing on the policing needs of our old people's homes.

Naughtie: Thank you, Charlotte. And now, let's test the mood down there in Melton Mowbray. Sarah, how are the ordinary voters reacting to these new proposals?

Quin: Well, Jim, there's hardly anyone around yet here, because it's still a bit early. But I can see one or two lights coming on in the block of flats across the road.

Naughtie: That's fascinating, Sarah. But how do you think the people of Shepton Mallet would react if they had got up and were there talking to you? Can you get a feel at all of how these proposals are playing, in what has been singled out as one of the top 234 key marginals?

Caroline: Well, Jim, what you have to remember is that this is one of the top 234 key marginal seats, and it is what the voters here think that will decide who enters Downing Street on the 6th of May.

Oh, I think there's someone coming! Hang on, excuse me, sir, could you tell us...

Naughtie: ...very interesting, Caroline. Don't go away. We'll be coming back to you when more people have got up! And now it's just coming up to 7.20, and it's time for a look at the papers. And there's no agreement on the main story. Here's the Independent, with a picture of Charles Kennedy, who will today be visiting a pre-primary school in Stoke Poges.

The Telegraph leads on Michael Howard's crackdown on traditional rural skills. And the Guardian tells us that the Prime Minister is going for the grey vote, when he visits an old people's home to talk about policing.

And, finally, the Daily Mail has an amusing cartoon by Mac, showing Robert Kilroy-Silk painting on a wall the words "Kilroy was here".

John Humphrys *(for it is now he)*: Thank you, Jim. And now today is an important day for some of the smaller parties in this election, who will be unveiling their manifestos, telling us what they will be doing when they're in government.

And round the table we've got Hewell Hywell from Plaid Cymru, Jethro Trescothick, deputy leader of the Cornish Independence Party, Shona Spinach, who is a spokesperson for the Greens Party, and, finally, Dave Blackshirt from the British Nice Party, which believes in the repatriation of everyone except himself.

Shona, could I come to you first? The chances of you getting any votes at all in this election are, frankly, nil. So why are you bothering? It's all a bit pointless, isn't it?

Shona *(sobbing)*: Well, you asked me to come on.

Humphrys: Well, that's all we've got time for from the smaller parties. Later in the programme I shall talking to Aqbal Al Mahd, leader of the Death To George Galloway, Oona King And Everyone Else Party. But, first, we're going back to Sarah in Haywards Heath. What's the atmosphere like down there in Essex, or Devon, or wherever it is?

Quin: Well, John, I'm now standing in the middle of a busy shopping centre in this quiet north country village, and I have to say that there is very little sign of election fever in what is one of the top 234 key marginals in the country. A car has just gone past, with a window sticker referring to the Prime Minister in a rather unflattering way!

Humphrys: Ha, ha, ha!

Quin: And I suppose we could take that as a pointer to the way the swing voters are leaning in this all-important inner city marginal. But I wouldn't want to read too much into it at this early stage.

Humphrys: Thank you, Caroline. And now it's 7.45 and here in the studio we have our old friend, Bob Worcester-Sauce, from the polling organisation Sori Wegotthatwrong. Bob, do you think the various initiatives we're going to see today from the party leaders – that's more police in old people's homes, a boost for traditional rural skills, better nutrition for the under-5s – is that going to make a difference, especially in those key 234 marginals that we keep hearing about?

Bertie Wooster: That's a fascinating question. I think what we're seeing overall at the moment is that there's very little movement from any of the 14 demographic social groups which we've identified as being the decisive swing factor in the days which remain before polling. For example, the Gay Over-70s were two weeks ago registering a very significant 32.7 percent support for the Lib Dems, but the most recent figure shows this as having declined to only 32.6 percent, which, if replicated across the country, could give the Scottish Nationalists a very real prospect...

Naughtie: ...I'll have to stop you there, Bob, because it's time for Charlotte Green to have another look at the papers.

Green: And there's no agreement on the main story. The Daily Telegraph has an exclusive about the Prime Minister's planned visit to an old policemen's home to talk about traditional skills for the under-5s and *(continued for 94 hours)*

Youthful apathy strikes the Peasants' Revolt

Truly Mad and Deeply Dishonest (18)

A WONDERFUL love story by Anthony Mingella (director of "The Scottish Impatient"). Tony and Gordon are deeply in love although one of them is dead. But which one is it? Viewers will weep at this moving portrayal of grief in high places.

Eye rating: ZZZZZZZZZZZZ

How Lord Birt Broke The News About His Marriage To Lady Birt

THE EYE PRINTS THE TELL-TALE EMAIL

Dear Lady Birt,

Having undergone a thorough re-evaluation of our long-term cohabitation structure, I regret to inform you that, as a result of a rationalisation process, your position as marital partner has become surplus to requirements.

This follows a more competitive bid for conjugal services submitted by the independent rival Mrs Eithne Penpusher who will be replacing you as of midnight Tuesday.

You are therefore required to empty all drawers, closets, bathroom cabinets, etc, and outsource yourself at once. Your co-operation in the above arrangements will be appreciated.

Signed,

J. Birt, Department of Very Blue Skies Thinking,
C/o 10 Downing Street.

The Secret DIARY OF SIR JOHN MAJOR KG aged 73¾

Monday

I was not inconsiderably pleased at breakfast to hear on the radio that I am to be a knight! And not an ordinary knight. Oh no. I am to be a Knight of the Garter which is, in my judgement, one of the most important knights you can be. As I said to my wife Norman over my bowl of chocolate-flavoured cinammon hoops with dried raspberries, "Only very famous and brave knights are given this great honour."

"Like Mrs Thatcher," she said in her usual unhelpful manner.

At this moment the phone rang and, naturally, I assumed that it would be someone from Buckingham Palace to tell me what colour to wear at the ceremony. (Grey, I think.)

"Hello," I said. "You are speaking to Sir John Major, Knight of the Garter, oh yes."

There was, however, a familiar voice at the other end of the phone.

"Hello, Sexy-pants," said Mrs Currie, for it was no less than she. "Congratulations! We had some fabulous Nights with Garters, didn't we, Big Boy?"

I was not inconsiderably incandescent with rage at being reminded of something which I had drawn a line under and from which I had made it clear that I had moved on.

"I think you have the wrong number, Mrs Currie," I said, thinking quickly, so that my wife Norman would not know who was on the phone.

© J. Major, 2005.

LABOUR ACCUSES TORIES OF 'PARTY POLITICS'

by Our Political Staff **Peter O'Bore**

A FURIOUS government spokesman hit out last night at Conservative election tactics.

"There are some things," he said, "that are too important to play party politics with. And one of those is the election."

Vote Labour

He continued, "It's bad enough trying to score party political points about the economy, or the health service, but to introduce party politics into the general election represents a new low."

He concluded, "When it comes to something as vital as a democratic election, surely the whole country can put aside its political differences and unite behind the government."

"In my day, kids used to walk to school!"

What You Missed
That Paxman-Blair Showdown In Full

Paxman: Prime Minister, the question all the voters want answered at this election is, "How long is a piece of string?"

Blair: Well, Jeremy, there simply isn't an easy answer to that one.

Paxman: But you have some idea?

Blair: No, what we've done is looked at the string very carefully, and looked at ways of measuring it.

Paxman: So, you've no idea, have you?

Blair: It's not a question of having an idea.

Paxman: What are we talking – inches? Feet? Yards? Miles?

Blair: I don't think it's helpful to speculate. The fact is that...

Paxman: So, you've no idea?

Blair: Look, the previous government had no idea of the length of...

Paxman: Oh come on, you've been in power for eight years. You must have some idea by now.

Blair: Look, Jeremy, I've told you – and I come back to this – there's no point in talking about lengths. We're looking at both ends of the string and... er... that's what needs to be done.

Paxman: So you've no idea at all, not even the foggiest clue, as to the length of a piece of string.

Blair: No, what I am saying, and I am saying this quite specifically, is that the length of a piece of string is not just something I can come on here and tell you. Er... it doesn't work like that.

Paxman: Don't know, don't know, don't know, ha, ha, don't know, don't know *(continues all night)*.

★ BAGHDAD TIMES ★

Friday 29 April 2005

VIOLENCE OVERSHADOWS ELECTION

by Our Man In London A.A. Gilgamesh

ANY HOPE that the British elections would pass off peacefully was shattered by the horrifying explosion of violence which has erupted in the eastern suburbs of the capital city, London.

Huge mobs of fanatical Islamic extremists have roamed the streets, issuing death threats to the handful of candidates who have been brave enough to stand for election, in a bid to restore democracy to Britain after years as a one-party state.

A particular target of the insurgent gangs has been George Galawi, a loyal supporter of dictator Saddam Hussein, who now runs the Shite Party, and who has faced repeated death threats for daring to stand up for Iraq against the imperialist aggressors.

Babylondon

Another victim of this sea of sectarian violence is the candidate of the official ruling party, Oona King, who has tried to promote multi-ethnic tolerance in this troubled city by being the first ever white, black, female, Jewish Muslim since Michael Jackson.

O Little Town of Bethnal Green

In fact, things in London have got so bad that the city's mayor, Ken Livingstone (known to his millions of followers as Salamander the Magnificent), can only travel in a bullet-proof vehicle, surrounded by armed guards.

So much for democracy British-style.

"The off switch is on the blink again..."

62

The Daily Telegraph

Habemus Papam!!

Rottweilerus Electus Ab Conclavo Cardinalibus

PER NOSTRUM HOMINEM IN VATICANO MARTINUS NOVATERRA, EDITORE TELEGRAPHII QUOTIDIANI

GAUDEAMUS deo gratia! Milliones pilgrimes Catholici exultaverunt in piazza Sancti Petri quando puffum fumi candidi ascendavit in caelum quam signum collegium cardinalorum electaverunt novum papam.

Cardinalis Rolandratticus est primus pontifex Germanicus in tempore modernus. **(Full story in English, see other newspapers.)**

The Grauniad

World Horrified As Catholic Is Made Pope

Polly Toynbee
Our Woman in Islington

In what will be remembered as one of the most catastrophic blunders in history, the Catholic church yesterday turned its back on the modern world by electing a white male as Pope, when the whole world was crying out for the choice of a black woman from the developing world.

And worse still – the new so-called Pope of Rome is an unashamed Catholic, who unashamedly champions such antediluvian views as a belief in God.

In what will be viewed as a slap in the face for the world's 1.5 trillion committed atheists *(cont'd p. 94)*

The Sun

PAPA NAZI!

First-Ever Nazi Wins Pope Idol

by Our Man Watching Sky TV

THE SUN can exclusively reveal that a former top SS man yesterday seized power in a Papal coup that has left the world's 1.5 billion Catholics shocked and stunned.

Cardinal Rottweiler, 78, the newly crowned Pontiff, is far from being the humble man of God he

likes to pretend to be.

In fact he was one of Hitler's top henchmen, intimately involved in planning World War Two.

No wonder he has taken the name Benito XVIII, in honour of his childhood hero Mussolini, the Fascist dictator who ruled Italy with a rod of iron.

Believers are appalled that *(cont'd p. 94)*

Daily Mail

NEW BLAIR GAFFE PUTS TORIES 10 POINTS AHEAD!!

by Our Man in
Cloud-Cuckoo Land
Paul Dacre

TONY BLAIR'S outrageous lies have yet again made a Tory win a racing certainty.

At a press conference yesterday, the prime minister shocked his audience by saying "Good morning" when anyone present could see with their own eyes that the rain was pouring down outside and that it was in fact not a very

"good morning" at all.

This shameless lie spells the end for the conman Blair, whose inability to tell the truth on any subject has finally convinced Britain's 10.5 million Labour supporters that they should commit suicide tomorrow morning rather than go to the polls and *(cont'd p. 94)*

THE Sun

Friday, May 13, 2005

EXCLUSIVE

'I'M AT IT ALL THE TIME!' Says PM

By TREVOR BEARD
Chief Political Editor

IN AN astonishingly frank exclusive interview with the Sun newspaper, Tony Blair yesterday boasted that he does it "five times a night".

As his wife Cherie giggled in the background, Britain's longest-serving Labour premier went on, "I can do it any time I like, and then do it again."

It is rare for a prime minister to admit so openly to his passion for lying.

But Tony Blair makes no bones about it. "I'm a normal guy, look, I like lying. I don't see anything to be ashamed of."

Lies Matters

At this point, wife Cherie chipped in with a saucy comment of her own. "Size matters," she said, "and when it comes to a good lie, the bigger the better, I say.

"And I don't mind telling you that Tony's are whoppers!"

The happy couple then cuddled up to each other, as if to prove Tony's claim that his health problems have not impaired his ability to "make it up" at all times of the day or night.

Tony then told us the moving story of how the late Pope had personally insisted on flying to Chequers to bless Tony and Cherie's marriage on their 25th wedding anniversary.

General Erection

"No, he didn't," Cherie butted in. "You're at it again, you naughty boy! Oo-er, there's no stopping you, is there, once you get going?"

Feeling that I was one too many for the party, I tiptoed towards the door and left the two of them lying contentedly together.

© The Rupert Murdoch 'Re-elect Tony' Campaign 2005.

ELECTION FRAUD

"Because it's a secret ballot, you're not allowed to find out who you voted for"

VE DAY –
ANNIVERSARY SOUVENIR

The Daily Private Eye

MAY 6 2005   PRICE 12/6½

VICTORY!!!

❖

NATION FAILS TO CELEBRATE AS WAR PREMIER IS NOT CHEERED BY MILLIONS

NO ONE ORGANISES STREET PARTIES IN SPONTANEOUS OUTBURST OF APATHY

No crowd filled the Mall yesterday to acclaim moment of victory

"Victory is ours!" a triumphant Prime Minister told the nation last night, but since everyone had long since gone to bed, no one was listening.

After five long weeks of gruelling political warfare, the last shots had been fired and the whole nation breathed a collective sigh of relief.

NEW ERA YAWNS

In Piccadilly Circus, at the heart of London's West End, an eerie silence greeted the historic news.

From Eros the streets in all directions were deserted. A lone taxi-driver, Sid Montgomery-Massingberd said, "I've never known nothing like this. I blame Red Ken and his congestion charge."

The story was the same across the nation. Old-age pensioners slept openly in their beds, as teenagers danced the night away under the influence of Class A drugs.

HOW WE SUFFERED

"It's over at last," said a typical East End housewife, Mrs Sonali Onanugu. "Now we can get on peacefully with our lives, without dreading round-the-clock bombardment of leaflets, loudspeakers and George Galloway coming to the door telling us that the Koran is his favourite bedside reading."

Meanwhile huge crowds packed into the nearby Ferret and Trombone (formerly the Duke of Cambridge), cheering wildly as they watched the Champions' League Semi-final.

QUEEN RECEIVES HISTORIC TELEGRAM

Her Majesty the Queen last night personally received an historic telegram from her prime minister.

"I am proud to report to your Majesty that I have secured a complete and crushing victory over all our opponents. I therefore have the honour to be prime minister of this country, and would like to invite you to stay on as Queen for the next five years.

God Save Myself!
Winstony Blairchill
P.S. No need for you to come out on the palace balcony. Cherie and I will do that one.

Victory in Election special

Daily ✦ Mail

FRIDAY, May 6, 2005

BLAIR CRUSHED IN HOWARD'S NIGHT OF VICTORY

By Our Political Staff
Paul Dacresofspacetofill

NO WONDER Tony Blair's face was white with shock as the news filtered through that he had won a historic third term.

Blair could baredly conceal his humiliation at the final announcement that Michael Howard's Conservatives had romped home to defeat.

House Prices Will Fall

Blair's faltering speech gave the game away as he smiled and waved to his supporters after the devastating blow of winning with a 67-seat majority began to take its toll.

Immigration Will Rise

The scale of Mr Howard's victory was immediately apparent when the Tory leader told weeping Party workers, "I resign."

FULL STORY pp. 2, 3, 4, 5, 6, 7, 94

PAXMAN INTERVIEWS GOD

Paxman *(for it is he)*: Not going too well, is it?

God *(for it is He)*: Er…

Paxman: It's a bloody disaster, isn't it? War, Famine, Plague, Death. Not a pretty picture.

God: Well, er…

Paxman: Come on, really! You have to have a better answer than that. Your opponent is just running away with it…

God: You see, I…

Paxman: No, no, that's not good enough. Let's face it, you're just an old bearded has-been who should just pack it in…

(Continues all night)

THE COUNT AT FOLKESTONE & HYTHE

POETRY CORNER

Lines On Hearing The First Bluebell Of Spring by David Blunkett, the former Home Secretary and People's Poet Laureate

Bluebells are blue,
Labour is red.
Can I have my job back?
(That's enough. Ed.)

E.J. Blunkett
(17½ lovechildren)

"HOORAY! We all lost!"

NEW CRONY ROW ROCKS LABOUR

by Our Political Staff
Luke Skynews

ACCUSATIONS of 'cronyism' were being thrown around the Galaxy last night as it emerged that Anakin Skywalker had been made Lord Vader solely because he was a friend of Tony Blair.

Rumours that Annekin Skywalker had donated a large cheque to the Imperial fighting fund shortly before being ennobled were hotly denied by a spokesman for Lord Vader, Mr Sith.

Said Mr Sith, "Lord Vader was given the title on merit. Just as he was given the contract to

Lord Vader

create a clone army to wipe out the universe. It is nothing to do with rewarding favours."

OBE-Wan Kenobi

A spokesman for Mr Blair added, "This is a very old story. It all happened a long, long time ago in a galaxy far, far away".

A long-time critic of Lord Vader, Mr Yoda, added, "To the dark side, Tony Blair has gone".

"How much longer before you stop and ask for directions, Brian?"

Let's Parlez Barclais!

Lesson 94
Dans Les Courts

Justice Coqauvin (*pour c'est lui*): Bonjour, Monsieur Barclais et Monsieur Barclais. Que voulez-vous?

Les Frères Barclais (*ensemble*): Un writ, s'il vous plait, pour Le Temps de Londres et le Dirty Digger.

Justice Coqauvin: Mais, pourquoi vous ne suez pas en Angleterre?

Les Frères Barclais: Parce que we might lose!

Justice Coqauvin: Vouse êtes un véritable pair de lunes.

Les Frères Barclais: Bâtard! Nous allons suez VOUS as well!!

Justice Coqauvin: Retournez a votre château sur l'île de Brilleau tout de suite or je senderai vous à prison pour le reste de votre life!

Les Frères Barclais: Boo hoo hoo hoo la la.

(Le case continue)

WHO ARE THEY?
The Frontrunners To Succeed Michael Howard

DAVID DAVID, 57. Hotly tipped to take the Tory hot-seat, David David is a high-flying man in a suit of whom you have never heard. **Evens favourite**.

LIAM FOX, 43. Currently Shadow Spokesman for Shadow Spokesmen, Fox has a suit and flies high. Friends say that they have never heard of him. **Odds 7/2**.

MALCOLM RIFKIND. Intensely old at 58, Rifkind is unlikely to become leader, due to the age of his suit and his tendency to wear spectacles. Friends say that despite being a Scotsman he is not known for flying – either high or low. **Odds 10/1**.

MICHAEL GOVE, 17½. Intensely intense, Gove is part of the young "Nottingham set", whose aim is to "wear suits, fly high and have some friends". **Odds 50/1**.

JUSTINE TOTTY, 21. Dark horse after her surprise victory at Putney, Totty represents the new face of young Toryism. She rejects spectacles and favours a two-piece suit and will appear on the front page of the Telegraph. **Odds 100/1**.

MR INCREDIBLE, 49. Red-suited, retired super-hero now hoping to start flying again and return to active politics as leader of the Conservatives *(Cont. p. 94)*

CANDIDATES FOR CONSERVATIVE RACE MAKE THEMSELVES KNOWN

"Well, that was a load of Sith"

The Daily Telegraph

BRITAIN'S BEST-SELLING QUALITY DAILY   Friday, May 27, 2005

Galloway Humiliated At Senate Hearing – 'MP Clearly Guilty' Says Everyone

By Our Washington Staff Lunchtime O'Bias

THE controversial MP for Bethnal Green, Mr George Galloway, suffered a devastating reverse yesterday in front of a distinguished group of American senators.

The pathetic Galloway, when confronted by the razor-sharp questioning of New Dworkin senator Kermit Moosejaw, could only speak for twenty minutes without notes while listing the errors in Mr Moosejaw's report.

So feeble was the MP's self-justification that the senators could only listen in silence, occasionally breaking down and weeping, as Mr Galloway proved that they had copied the whole report out of the Daily Telegraph.

ON OTHER PAGES

Senator Moosejaw: Will this brilliant advocate be the next President of the United States? **2** Will Galloway have to kill himself after this debacle? **3**

PLUS!

Sudailytelegraph

The fiendish new game where you sue us for huge sums of money. Just fill in the numbers!

£	9	9	9	9	9	9

WHOOPS! I FORGOT TO PUT MY LIGHTSABRE ON 'CHARGE'

BESTIE

BLUNKETT TO BE FAST-TRACKED TO SAINTHOOD

by Our Man In The Vatican **Lunchtime O'Pus-Dei**

THE newly elected Pope, Antonio I, yesterday confirmed that he had fast-tracked a blind holy man, the Blessed Blunkett, to instant sainthood.

Traditionalists protested that the Blessed Blunkett did not meet the strict conditions for sainthood laid down by the Church.

One important disadvantage is that the bearded English mystic (surely 'misfit'? Ed) is still alive, whereas it has hitherto been a rule that a saint must be dead.

Shock

But supporters of his claim to sanctity point out that Blunkett was kind to dogs, married women and children, many of whom he claimed were his own.

Most important of all, critics point out that saints are required to have performed at least two genuine miracles, and claim that there is no evidence of Blunkett having performed the necessary supernatural acts.

Spokesmen for Pope Blairnedict the 94th insist, however, that the Blessed Blunkett has indeed performed two astonishing and fully attested miracles in the past few months alone.

Firstly, he has got his job back in the Cabinet. And, secondly, he has managed to make Charles Clarke look like a halfway competent Home Secretary.

Lines written by the Rt Hon David Blunkett MP on his reappointment as a Cabinet Minister with responsibilty for the Child Support Agency.

Labour is red,
The Tories are blue.
I've got my job back,
So sod all of you.

D. Blunkett, The People's Poet
(17½ lovechildren)

THE Sun SAYS

THE news that Malcolm Glazer has been allowed to take a controlling share in Manchester United is one that naturally will horrify all Sun readers, who will be appalled by the fact that an American citizen with no real knowledge of day-to-day life in Britain can be allowed to get away with buying the Sun. (Surely 'Manchester United'? Ed.)

How can an American like Mr Murdoch *(Surely Mr Glazer? Ed.)*, who pays no taxes in this country and who will almost certainly treat the fans with contempt, be allowed to turn this symbol of Britain abroad into his own personal cash cow for Sky TV *(You're fired. Rupert)*.

SUN-DOKU!

THE fiendishly hard new puzzle that's gripping the whole nation – specially adapted for our readers. Remember all the numbers from 1 to 9 must be placed in the box. Happy puzzling!

1	2	3
4	5	6
7	8	

EXCLUSIVE TO ALL PAPERS

FAMOUS WOMAN HAS CANCER

On Other Pages

● Pictures of the famous woman who has cancer with less famous boyfriend who doesn't have cancer **2-17**

● Pictures of famous woman in skimpy tops **18-37**

● Pictures of millions of other women who aren't famous with cancer *(cancelled due to lack of space)*

PLUS

● 'I've Had It Too' by lots of female journalists **37-63**

● 'What Happens When Famous People Get Cancer' by Dr Thomas Utterfraud **94**

FOOTBALLER NOT ARRESTED

THE sporting world was in a state of shock following the incredible news that a footballer failed to spend a night in the cells.

An FA spokesman said, "It's a shame when professional footballers fail to make the headlines for all the wrong reasons – at the end of the day these people are role models to millions of juvenile delinquents and... *(cont. p. 94)*

THE Sun

Friday, May 27, 2005

★ Name the mystery Piano Man and win Wayne Rooney's FA Cup-Losing Jockstrap! p. 94

TYRANT IN

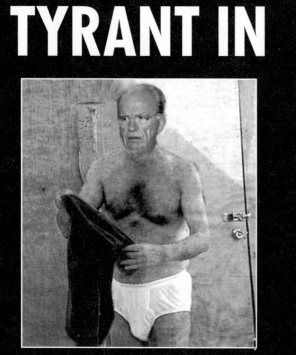

UNDERPANTS

AT LAST we can show you the pathetic sight of the world's most hated man in his undies.

Once he was feared by millions – now we see him as he really is. A sad old man in his Y-fronts.

But don't feel sorry for him. It is all his own fault for inflicting such misery on the millions of *(cont. p. 94)*

Christopher Robin Hoodie

"Let's go and hang about on the footbridge"

*What f***ing great big teeth you've got, Grandma*

—LITTLE RED RIDING HOODIE—

Nursery Times

············· Friday, 10 June, 2005 ·············

ASBO SERVED ON GOLDILOCKS SHOCK

by **Hans Muslim Anderson**

A SEVEN -year-old girl who broke into a woodland cottage owned by the Bear family has become the latest subject of an anti-social behaviour order.

The court heard that once inside the cottage the little girl had "run amok", stealing porridge, breaking chairs and finally squatting in one of the bedrooms.

Said Mr Bear, "It was every bear's worst nightmare. We came back from our afternoon walk to find that the cottage had been trashed." He continued, "You never think it is going to happen to you. We are still coming to terms with our trauma and we are all going to family therapy."

Goldilocks, however, refused to accept responsibility for her actions. "I blame my parents," she continued, "for failing to teach me the difference between right and left."

Her mother, Mrs Waynetta Goldilocks, who has 15 other children and lives in an old shoe, said, "I don't know what to do. Basically Goldilocks is a good girl but I blame the school for failing to teach her that she should have nicked all the cutlery rather than just eating the *(contd. p. 94)*

On Other Pages
● Yellow Brick Road – new toll charge **1** ● Peter Pan rushed to hospital following sex charge verdict. **2**
● Neighbour illegally cut down Giant Beanstalk – "It spoilt my view" he says **94**

Very Late News

Sheriff of Nottingham to outlaw Robin Hoodie by Piers 'Ye Moron' Plowman

Ye Sheriff of Nottingham hath vowed to (cont 1194)

POLLY FILLER

Pregnancy Diary

In the first of a series of extracts from her new book Give Me The Mummy!*, Polly Filler*

chronicles her sometimes hilarious but always moving struggle to have a baby.

WE always knew, from the first time we went to the doctor, that we were going to have problems.

There we were, the useless Simon and I, in the surgery, when our GP opened the test results. It was my worst fear. "Polly," he said kindly, "there's nothing wrong with you or Simon. You'll probably have a baby immediately."

My heart pounded. How was I going to make a whole book out of my pregnancy problems? The opportunity of producing a soul-searching yet humorous account of my fertility woes had been cruelly snatched away from me.

As tears streamed down my face, the doctor coolly sat us down and went through the options.

He suggested that during my "fertility windows" the useless Simon should spend more time watching Celebrity Chelsea Tractor Racing from Sloane Square, presented by A.A. Clarkson and Jeremy Gill, to make sure that he wasn't in the mood for sexual intercourse at the right time in my cycle!

And, if things got desperate and I was *really* in the mood, Simon had to be prepared to hop on his moped and travel to the other side of town to play five-a-side football with his mates, so there was no possible danger of premature conception.

NINE months later – success! Out popped my book, weighing in at a healthy seven pounds (and ninety-nine pence!), charting in excruciating gynaecological detail the trials and tribulations of our efforts at conception.

And, you know what was the most painful part of the whole gory process? Writing the foreword where I tried to justify the book on the grounds that millions of ordinary women saw me as a role model and I thought that it would help them in their own pregnancies! Ouch! Still, it was all worth it!

As my partner, the useless Simon always says, "It's Pukka Chekka!" and "Lovely Lolly".

TOMORROW: Polly and Simon go through exactly the same things as everyone else when they have a baby.

© Polly Filler, The Daily Telegraph, the Daily Mail etc etc.

EYE BUY

10 of the best

No. 94 COATHANGERS Chosen by Philippa Page

No Frills

Asda's "Eezihang", made in China from PVC, bravely sticks to the traditional design. 99p

Durable

M&S have come up with a new range of long-lasting Italian-style hangers, the "Milano", the "Torino" and the "Seville". £9.99 for set of three.

Upmarket

The "Coathanger's coathanger", the "Burlington" is a superbly engineered Finnish design made from rainforest teak. Only available from Piltdown's of Jermyn Street. £59.99.

Going away?

The "Traveller-De Luxe" from Monty's of Crouch End is a revolutionary new concept in coathangers, folding away into the size of a cigarette packet when not in use. £19.99.

Top of the Range

The "Highgrove", marketed by the Duchy of Cornwall (all profits to charity) is hand-made in Poundbury, Dorset, to an 18th century design by Quinlan Terry. Six-month waiting list. £325.99 (plus p&p).

Free 'n easy

Perhaps the best-value of all, this ultra-basic hanger is given away free to all customers of the fast-expanding Mr Staingone dry-cleaning chain. *(That's enough coathangers, Ed.)*

What are you in for?

Graffiti

"Lulus, Sir. Thousands of them."

OUI, IT'S NON!!!

by Our European Staff
Russel Sprout

YES, IT'S 'NO'! That was the shock message that rang out yesterday from Calais to Carcassonne, from Limoges to Lille, from Bordeaux to Biarritz *(That's enough French towns. Ed.)*

The French people have delivered their verdict!

In the biggest upset since the French revolutionaries stormed the Bastille and chopped the head off their king, the people of this proud and ancient land have delivered the most almighty snub to their ruling class since the French revolutionaries stormed the *(You've done this bit. Ed.)*

And the message could not be clearer! From Calais to Caen, from Montpellier to Marseilles, from Dijon to Mustard *(Get on with the clear message. Ed.)*

The French nation has spoken with one clear, unequivocal voice.

'Non!,' they have said. Which is the French for 'no'. And they mean it!

So what is it that they are saying 'no' to?

Who cares?! All that matters is that they have said no.

And as I sit here on the top of the Eiffel Tower, gazing down at a sea of happy, laughing, pretty Parisiennes, holding up their banners which proudly proclaim that one immortal word 'non', I realise that I have no idea what I am talking about!

© *All newspapers.*

WHY 'NON' MEANS 'OUI' Chirac Explains

by Our French Correspondent **Paris Hilton**

A SMILING President Chirac appeared on state television last night to proclaim his 'unqualified delight' at the verdict of the French people on the EU Constitution.

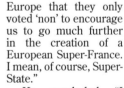

"In no way," he said, "is this a vote against Europe or the Constitution. In no way is it a vote against me.

"Rather," went on M. Chirac, "it is a perfectly understandable expression of dissatisfaction with the useless little man I appointed prime minister, M. Raffarindum, whom I have therefore sacked.

"In fact, it is quite obvious that the French people are so keen on Europe that they only voted 'non' to encourage us to go much further in the creation of a European Super-France. I mean, of course, Super-State."

He concluded, "I thank you with all my heart for this resounding vote of confidence in myself. I look forward to seeing you all again when we have another referendum again soon under our charismatic new prime minister, M. Cruella de Villepin *(Surely Dominique de Lawson? Ed.)*.

"Vive la France et, in the words of that Great Frenchman Louis XIV, 'le super-état c'est moi'."

NEE MEANS JA

by Our Man Who Hasn't A Clue What's Going On **Van der Vote**

HERE, in the land of windmills, clogs and tulips, the people of this tiny corner of the mighty European Union woke up today to find that they had voted 'njop' *(Please check. Ed.)* **and thrown the whole of the Continent into a seething cauldron of uncertainty and chaos.**

From Harlem to the Hague, from Rotterdam to Rembrandt, from Douwe Egbert to Haagen Dazs, the the message could not have been clearer.

"While we love Europe," said one tulip seller in Amsterdam, "we don't want to be part of it."

His sentiments were echoed by a cannabis grower from the little town of Spliff. "We Dutch," he said, "are a proud people, and we want to run our own affairs."

For the bewildered, bloody-nosed bureaucrats of Brussels, this has been the nightmare they never dreamed could happen, as news of the overwhelming 'Njej' sank in.

Said one senior official on the 89th floor of the Commission headquarters, "Of course we wholeheartedly respect the democratically expressed views of the Dutch nation, but we will press ahead with our plans regardless. It is what the Dutch people would really want, if only they were better informed."

As I cycled down one of Amsterdam's legendary canals in the autumn sunshine, I was surrounded by hordes of young clog-sporting Dutch girls asking me whether I would like a nice time.

The answer was, of course, a resounding 'jeh'!

The 'Oui' List In Full

A Guide To Those World-Famous French Celebs Who Led The Campaign To Accept The New EU Constitution

Maurice Chevalier	**Jules**
Edith Piaf	**Jim**
M. Hulot	**Asterix The European**
Jean-Paul Sartre	

(That's enough French celebrities. Ed.)

CRAZY FROG RING TONE

Non! Non! Non! Non! Non!

CRAZY TONE RINGS FROG

Ha! Ha! Ha! Jacques!

"Apparently in Europe they have 37 different words for 'No'!"

THE Sun SAYS

An Apology

In recent years we may on occasion have given the impression that we were not wholehearted admirers of our French neighbours across the Channel.

Headlines such as 'Hop Off Frogs', 'Frog Off You Garlic-Eating, Wine-Guzzling Onion-Sellers' and 'Who'd Bed A French Bird Who Smells Of Old Cheese And has Hairy Armpits?' may have led readers to believe that we in some way held the people of France in less than total affection and respect.

We now realise that, on the contrary, our French cousins are without doubt the most brave, perceptive, honourable and altogether delightful nation on God's earth.

We offer them our deepest apologies for any confusion which may have arisen, and call on our readers to travel at once to this wonderful country by Eurostar, fill their white vans with cheap lager and fags and salute the most admirable race of people who have ever rallied at the last minute to support Mr Murdoch's policy on Europe.

© *The Times.*

KINNOCK DEFENDS EU CONSTITUTION

What's wrong with being long-winded, incomprehensible and rejected by the voters?

The Man Whose Hour Has Come

The collapse of the European project has one unexpected beneficiary. The Conservative Party is now free to choose as its next leader the one man who can hope to guide them to victory at the next election. Now that the people of Europe have firmly rejected the Euro-federalist dream, this is surely the time for a committed Europhile like Mr Clarke to take over. *(Is this right? Ed.)*

© *All newspapers.*

Letters *to the Editor*

My Views on Tory Leadership from Sir John Major KG

SIR – I was not inconsiderably incandescent with rage when I read your article alleging that I was attempting to influence the election for a new leader of the Conservative Party. I would like to make it in no small measure clear that I did no such thing. Oh no! The suggestion that I am in any way attempting to "stop" Mr. Davis (or indeed any other candidate) is, in my judgement, unforgivable and contrary to the facts. I very specifically went out of my way to avoid saying that Mr Davis should be "stopped". Nor did I hint that Mr Clarke with his very considerable talents and experience, would be an ideal choice to unite the party and to appeal to all those voters in the centre of British politics, whose support will be essential if we are ever again to win an election as I did in 1992. What I did say was that, while in no way favouring any candidate above the others, and let me make it clear, we have at least 28 excellent candidates, all of whom would make superb leaders of the party, in the end the only thing that matters is that the party should choose the right candidate for the job, i.e. Mr Clarke and not Mr Davis
Sir John Major (not 'Mr' as some people still mistakenly address me!)
Greystroke, Grays Inn Road, Grays, Essex

RADIO FOUR

What You Missed

Ken Clarke's All-Time Jazz Greats presented by the Rt Hon Kenneth Clarke MP PC

Kenny Clarke: Hi there, hepcats! And let's groove with a few of the good old good ones from the hot hits of yesteryear!

It's often said that the good die young. And that's never more true than in jazz. I'm thinking of such legends as Jelly-Roll Major, Hotlips Hague, Pinetop Duncan Smith and, of course, Count Michael Howard whose career ended so tragically with a stake through his heart.

But let's start with one of the great classics in the history of the 'Blues' – Fats Soames's immortal *I'm Gonna Sit Right Down And Write Myself A Letter Of Resignation.*

(Boring jazz music plays for a short while until presenter gets bored and wishes to hear sound of own voice)

Clarke: Wasn't that great? But now, from the golden age of dance bands, the legendary 1922 Committee recording of *Hullo Central Office, Give Me Doctor Liam Fox.*

(Further short snatch of scratchy old 78)

Clarke: Mmmmm – jazz! And we end today with that larger-than-life genius with his cigar, his pint of bitter and his legendary trademark Hush Puppies. Who better to blow his own trumpet than the 'King' himself – Kenny Clarke, legendary bluesman and next leader of the Conservative Party.

(Long excerpt of man blowing own trumpet)

Clarke: Well, that's all we have time for today, all you kool kats and beboppers. Next week I'll be playing records by Ted Heath & His Washed-Up Band, Thelonious 'Mad Monk' Joseph and the Normo Tebbs Hot Five – but none by Miles 'David' Davis. Stay cool, and remember – Vote Tory!

BLAIR'S ASTONISHING FINAL LEGACY

Those 94 Bills which will guarantee Blair's place in the history books.

Retirement Homes Bill

The Government will take steps to ensure that in future all old people's homes will be required to install stairlifts, even if they are bungalows.

The Road Safety (Amendment) Bill

Anyone caught smoking while at the wheel of a car, even if it is stationary, will be liable to an on-the-spot fine of £1000, or 100 hours of community service.

The Maternity Benefit Extension Bill

A Bill to entitle single women without children to claim maternity benefit.

The Protection of Landlords and Civil Disturbances Bill

A Bill to entitle landlords the right to refuse to sell drink to customers whose clear aim is to become intoxicated.

The Sandwich Board Bill

The Government is to set up a new agency to regulate the size, shape and content of sandwiches (not including baguettes).

The Prohibition of Canine Waste Bill

Magistrates will be empowered to imprison all dogs found fouling public spaces (not including cemeteries) where their owners have not acted promptly to remove the offending material (15 mins max Monday to Friday 7am – 7pm).

The Tree and Shrub Registration Bill

Householders occupying domestic premises will be required to register with their local authority any tree or shrub growing on their land above a height of 3.2 metres (3mm for bonsai species).

The Incitement to Hatred of Blunkett Bill

A Bill to make it a criminal offence to criticise or in any way defame the new Secretary of State for Work and Pensions or to impugn his integrity in such a way as to bring him into public ridicule. The penalty for this offence shall be death.

Anti-Social Behaviour Order (Extension) Bill

The following new offences will be made subject to the imposition of an ASBO:

1. The use of skateboards in hospital car parks.

2. The dropping of ring-pulls from drink cans in a public place.

3. The offering of Turkey Twizzlers to a minor.

4. Over-encouragement of urban pigeons by providing them with seed or other edible foodstuffs in excess of 1 kilogram.

5. The erection of a windfarm in a private garden without planning permission.

6. The use of personal stereo equipment in a place of worship in such a way as to inconvenience other members of the congregation.

7. The emission of excessive noise from the act of turning the pages of a book or periodical in bed while your partner is trying to sleep.

The Miscellaneous Provisions Bill

A Bill to abolish Magna Carta, the NHS, trial by jury, habeas corpus, state schools, etc.

That EU Crisis Dinner Menu In Full

French Whine

– ✳ –

Sour Kraut

– ✳ –

British Beef
(That's enough. Ed)

FA SECRETARY IN SEX SHOCK

Take a French letter, Miss Alam

"We are gathered here to celebrate the birth of little Asbo, named after his father who unfortunately is unable to be with us today"

'DEVIL IN CHURCH' SHOCK

by Our Media Staff **Stephen Glove**

THE WORLD of Fleet Street was gathered together for the last time yesterday, when hundreds of editors, politicians and people hoping for a job attended a service of thanksgiving at St Bride's Church to celebrate the end of the British newspaper industry.

The star guest was the man who had contributed most to that process, Mr Rupert Moloch, surrounded by a coven of imps and demons, including Ms Rebekah Witch and the late Kelvin McBeelzebub.

The Devil, dressed in a neat fireproof suit and showing no signs of his 7,380,000 million years, mounted the lectern to read a famous passage from his own version of what he introduced as 'the Bad Book'.

The lesson began:

"Let us now praise famous men and our fathers, who left us enough money to buy up pretty well every newspaper in this godforsaken little hole called Britain..."

At this point there was laughter from the assembled dignitaries, including most of the Cabinet, who were being prodded with forks by the aforementioned imps and demons.

The Rector of St Bride's, Canon Flannel, later led the congregation in a rousing selection of hymns, including "He's Got The Whole News Of The World In His Hand", "I've Got The Sun In The Morning And The Sky At Night" and "The Times They Are A-Changin' To A Tabloid".

A reception was later held at the Hellfire Club in Mayfair.

(Reuters. New address: Unit 317, The Trading Estate, Peterborough)

SUPERMODELS

KERBER

POETRY CORNER

In Memoriam James Doohan, better known as Chief Engineer Scott of *Star Trek* fame

So. Farewell then
"Scotty" – Chief
Engineer of the
USS Enterprise.

"Beam me up,
Scotty." That was
The catchphrase they
Used about you.

But now it
Is you who
Has been
Beamed up.

> Captain E.J. Thribb
> (Warp Factor 17½)

In Memoriam Richard Whiteley, host of television game show *Countdown*

So Farewell
Then Richard
Whiteley.

It is the
End of the
Countdown.

You have one
Vowel and
Two consonants.

R.I.P.

> E.J. Thribb
> (17½ times nightly)

In Memoriam Lord King of Wartnaby, former chairman of British Airways

So. Farewell
Then Lord King of Wartnaby.

You were Mrs Thatcher's
Favourite businessman.

Now you have passed Through the
Departure
Lounge and taken
Off into the
Heavens.

(Unless of course your
Flight has been
Delayed or even
Cancelled for
Operational reasons.)

> E.J. Thribb (£17½ single to Miami,
> airport taxes included)

The Secret DIARY OF SIR JOHN MAJOR KG aged 63¾

Monday

Today was in my judgement perhaps the most historic day even in my not inconsiderably historic life. Oh yes. Today, as I announced to my wife Norman at breakfast, in what I hope was a suitably historic voice, I am to become a "KG". "Oh yes?" she replied, "is that some sort of new breakfast

cereal?" – as usual completely missing the point. I had to inform her that, on the contrary, it is not a breakfast cereal at all, but a very important and ancient order of chivalry, going back to the Middle Ages and the days of the Grey Prince himself.

"How did you know that?" she asked. "Did you read it on the back of your cornflake packet?" "No," I rejoined,

becoming in no small measure somewhat irritated by her failure to recognise the importance of my historic day. "No," I told her. "If you must know, I looked it up on the internet. KG stands for Knight of the Garter, of which I have the very great honour to become one. Only Her Majesty herself is permitted to select the Knights, who must be 'brave, steadfast and pure of heart'."

"Well," said Norman. "It is just as well that she doesn't read the newspapers or your name might have been struck off."

Tuesday

My great day began extremely badly. I was trying on my special ceremonial robes, which I was just tucking into my trousers, when my brother Terry appeared at the door holding a new gnome he had made, dressed in identical robes to the ones I was currently donning.

"It's a 'Garter Gnome'," he announced. "D'you see – like 'Garden Gnome' except with 'Garter' instead of 'Garden'."

"Terry," I told him. "That is neither in any way funny or amusing."

"I was hoping you might give it to Her Majesty as a souvenir of your great day. And, by the way," he went on, "there is a special message written on the garter."

When I looked closely I saw the words "Thinking of you, big boy! Edwina". I was

beyond incandescence in my rage as I drove off in the specially hired mini-cab which was to drive me to the ceremony.

"What are you going as?" asked the driver, as we travelled in style down the M4. "Batman or what?"

I told him that, on the contrary, I was dressed as a Knight of the Garter and that should he wish to know more about it he should consult www.knightofthegarter.com on the "History Comes Alive" website. This shut him up, and he remained suitably chastened until we arrived at the historic Windsor Castle, where he said, "Shall I drop you here, squire, or will you fly the last bit?"

The procession was not inconsiderably impressive as I joined it, standing alongside none other than His Royal Highness the Duke of Edinburgh, who I recognised from his photographs in the paper. All around me was the flower of English chivalry, dressed in their finery. And there was I, one of them at last, one of the great and the good, with my specially designed coat of arms showing two biros rampant guarding a clipboard couchant superscribed with a parchment volume carrying the Gothic title 'Ye Booke Of Ye Bastards' over the motto 'Non inconsiderabile'.

Unfortunately, at that moment, who should I see bearing down on me but the woman whose name I never mention, i.e. Mrs Thatcher, also dressed as a Knightess of the Garter.

"Are you one of the new ones?" she cried out in her only too familiar voice. "It's funny, but you look just like that ghastly little man who they got to run the country after me and made such a mess of it."

GOVERNMENT WINS LOTTERY

by Our Lotto Staff **Ian Jackpot**

A SCOTTISH recluse living in central London today collected the biggest-ever lottery win on behalf of a syndicate known as 'New Labour'.

A smiling but dour Mr Gordon Brown received the cheque from Mrs Tessa Jowell, the well-known Hampstead celebrity, and told reporters, "I have been dreaming for years of getting my hands on this money. And now it is mine, all mine! Millions of it!"

What A Lottery I Got

Asked how he intended to spend the money, Mr Brown replied, "It will not change my way of life a scrap. I hope to spend it on schools and hospitals and all those things I would have to waste government money on.

"Now, thanks to my Lotto win [estimated odds 1 in 1], I won't have

to raise taxes quite as much as I'm going to have to do anyway."

Mr Brown admitted to reporters that he had ticked the box for "No Publicity" because he had not wanted the public to know that he had stolen all their money.

HOW DID THIS STORY GET INTO THE SUN – AGAIN?

Harry: Easy target for journalists (surely 'terrorists'? Ed)

by Our Special Correspondent **Andy Grenade**

DUE TO the appallingly lax security at News International, a fake story has yet again got into the Sun newspaper and has even appeared on the front page before anyone could stop it.

The story alleged that Prince Harry was at risk from a terrorist threat at the Royal Military Academy in Sandhurst.

But no check was made when it first tried to gain

admission to the paper and the story was waved through – despite the fact that it was absolutely clear that it was a 'dud'.

Tit and Bomb

Said editor Rebekah Wade, "We are taking this very seriously. We will do everything in our power to make sure it happens again".

ON OTHER PAGES
Blurred pictures of someone who might be Harry but probably isn't 2-94

'GREATEST SHOW ON EARTH' TO COINCIDE WITH WORLD SUMMIT

by Our Africa Staff **Phil Hyde-Park**

SOME of the world's top political names are to stage a rally in Edinburgh in order to "put pressure" on the scheduled meeting of global pop stars.

The rally is to be called G8 (a play on words from 'Live 8') and will be fronted by the charismatic guitar legend Tony Blair, of the band New Labour. Other top-lining acts promised for the historic gig include American legend George Bush of the Neocons, crooner Jacques Chirac and German Heavy Metal Industry front man Gerhard Schroeder.

Said Blair, "It's time we made these pop stars wake up to their responsibilities. After all, they are the ones who make things happen." He continued, "These people – like Geldof, Sting and the Spice Girls – are the most powerful people on the planet and it's high time they put Africa at

the top of their agenda."

Said Blair, "We're doing our bit, or rather we aren't, and the least these musicians could do is solve world poverty."

Said Sir Bob Geldof, "Fuck off!"

"I'm not sure that's helpful, Bob"

CAMILLA ON BALCONY

And, look – there's a big flying!

News in Brief
HUNDREDS OF IRAQIS NOT KILLED

THERE were astonishing scenes in Baghdad today, as hundreds of Iraqis gathered in a market square weren't killed in a suicide bombing.

"Not to have hundreds of innocent people killed in this way is something we could never have expected. Naturally we're all in a state of shock," said one local... *(cont. p. 94)*

FAMOUS MAN FOUND FAMOUS

THE WORLD of showbusiness was stunned by the news that a famous man has been found famous in an American court of law.

A spokesman for the Jackson family said, "Twelve good men and women true have proved what we always knew, that the famous man is very famous indeed, and *(cont. p. 94)*

BEST ARRESTED FOR SOMETHING OR OTHER

IT'S been revealed that police have arrested soccer legend George Best for something he's meant to have done.

On Other Pages
● Best Helps Police With Their Enquiries
● Best Helps Editors Fill Space

THIS WEEK

HUGH LAURIE

Do you have a favourite spoon?

I never feel my spoons are any good. I'm plagued with self-doubt about my collection. Are they really worth having? Or are people just being kind when they like my spoons. I don't know.

I gather your father was keen on spoons?

I was always a bit in awe of my father's spoons and I felt I could never live up to his example as a great spoon man. He was my hero spoon-wise.

You're a great success in America now. What are the spoons like over there?

It's been a bizarre experience for me. I never expected to be using American spoons and I keep thinking people are going to see through me and say, "You're a fraud. Stick to your English spoons buddy." But everyone's been very kind and I'm committed to American spoons for the next four years.

Your character, Dr Gregory House, what is his attitude to spoons?

He hates spoons. Almost as much as he hates patients. And yet here's the irony, his dislike of spoons doesn't stop him using them in emergency operations. But he has got a proper job, unlike me. I'm just an actor.

Has anything amusing ever happened to you in connection with a spoon?

You should really ask Stephen Fry this question. He would come up with a hilarious spoon anecdote because he is a genius and he can do everything. Act, write, direct, tell spoon stories. I'm just an actor. Er... do you mind if we leave it there, I'm feeling rather depressed now. Thank you.

NEXT WEEK: *Russell Crowe – "Me and My Crow".*

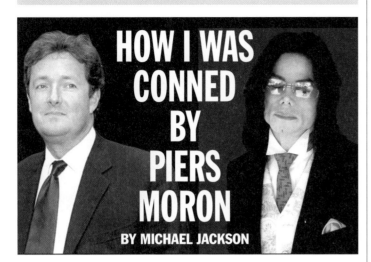

HOW I WAS CONNED BY PIERS MORON

BY MICHAEL JACKSON

IT was the most surreal encounter in all my mad years in the media. There I was on the end of a phone, talking to a man who claimed to be Piers Moron. And he was!

Amazingly, 'Moron' wanted to talk to me and I fell for it like a sucker. By turns earnest, flippant, self-pitying, joking, laughing, sobbing, 'Moro' tried to persuade me that he was really a great guy and not at all the moron that everyone claimed.

"They tell wicked lies about me, Michael," he said, in that little boy voice. "All that stuff about money and shares and photos and sex, but none of it is true. All I want to do is help people by telling their stories." He continued, "I have a talent which I want to share with the world. Does that make me a bad person?"

AND fool that I was, star-struck and naïve in the presence of such a global figure, I believed every word that Moron said.

Now I realise I was the victim of the master of manipulation and deceit. He sounded normal, but he is nothing more than a conman and I should never have got into bed with him.

© Michael Jackson 2005.

RADIO 3
WHAT YOU MISSED

Ken Clarke's All-Time Jazz Greats presented by the Rt Hon Kenneth Clarke MP PC

Kenny Clarke: Hi there again, hepcats! *(Lights up cigar and coughs violently for 10 minutes)* Welcome to part two of my all-time jazz greats. Today we're looking at some of the new names on the scene. And first The Moderniser Jazz Quartet, with Dave "Old Etonian" Cameron, George "Ozzie" Osborne, and, of course, "Wild" Mike Gove. Mmmm. Nice. So let's hear this cool track from their latest album, *The Notting Hill Experience.*

(Two minutes of boring music follows)

Clarke: Mmmm. Hopeless. Because, let's face it, the trouble with these youngsters today is that they can't compete with the giants of yesteryear. I'm thinking of Mad Mike Heseltine, Riffing "Mal" Rifkind and even the great Thatchmo herself.

So let's listen one more time to the Chingford Polecats' *On Yer Bike Blues* with Normo Tebbs on string 'em up bass.

(More dreary jazz music is played)

But there is still one name that everyone agrees is the King of Jazz, the grooviest groover, the heppest hep-cat of all – it's got to be Smokin' Ken Clarke!

So let's listen to my unforgettable recording of *Don't Step On My Old Brown Suede Hush Puppies* – and I don't have to tell you who is playing the trumpet. Smooth or what?

(We hear very old record with elderly man wheezing. Listeners switch off)

THE SHATTERED WORLD OF 'WACKO' LAWSON

by Our Showbiz Staff SARAH SANDWICH

TODAY the world of "Wacko" Lawson, the one-time golden boy of Sunday newspaper journalism, crashed in ruins.

At his £200 million Sussex ranch, Neveronsundaytelegraph-land, the blinds are drawn and no one is answering the door.

King of Pap

The legendary figure whose greatest hits included "I Discover Lord Lucan", "I Discover Lord Lucan Again" and "Pope To Wed Gay Partner", towered for 20 years over the industry that had given him fame and fortune.

But no more. Friends say he is "a shattered man". His weight is down to 26 stone, his face is a deathly shade of red and at times, says an intimate, "He scarcely seems to know where he is, or what he is doing".

Very Bad

"Wacko" Lawson, so called because of the countless stories about his bizarre and inappropriate behaviour, now faces an uncertain future.

Having been born into a leading showbiz family, Wacko found fame early when his father, Fatso Lawson (now Thinso), put him on the public stage alongside his sister Nigella.

They quickly became the nation's favourite showbiz double-act, until the raven-haired Nigella teamed up with her new partner Screaming Lord Saatchi.

He's History

Wacko began to live in a fantasy world of his own, convinced that one day he would achieve the supreme goal of editing the Daily Telegraph.

But it was not to be. Yesterday the jury of two, Fred and Dave Barclay, pronounced their unrelenting verdict – "you're fired".

And at a stroke, for one 46-year-old superstar, the clock stopped.

ON OTHER PAGES ● "I shouldn't have put paper to bed with bores in it," admits Lawso.

GLENDA SLAGG

THE GIRL YOU CAN'T GET TOO LITTLE OF!!

■ ANNE ROBINSON!?!?? Aren't-chasickofher?!? Everywhere you look, there she is a-grinnin' and a-gawpin' out at you from the paper – tellin' you how she's had a facelift, or she's selling her house, or she's battling some disease or other!!?! Who cares?! Cut it out, Anne – and I don't mean your nose!?! I'll tell you who's the Weakest Link!?!! *You* are! Goodbye!

■ HATS OFF to TV's Anne Robinson!?! The glamorous redhead who still looks great at 94?!? And she's brave enough to open her heart and tell us about the trials and torments of selling her house, having a facelift and battling a life-threatening disease!?! God bless you, Anne – you're an inspiration to us all!!?! (Thanks to you, my own house is now on the market!!?! 1 Bed, 1 Recep, Kitchen/Diner, Patio Garden overlooking railway. Offers over £6 million.)

■ JANE FONDA!?!! Aren'tcha-sickofher!?!! Telling us all that stuff about her miserable private life!?!! And doesn't she look terrible, considering that she's only 94!!?!

Barbarella??! More like Babar The Elephant!!?! Go back to Hanoi and bomb yourself?!!

■ JANE FONDA!?! I'm getting Fonda and Fonda of you!!? Geddit??! You're an inspiration to billions of women all over the world with your brave keep-fit videos and your inspirational books about your miserable private life!?! Gawd bless you, Jane!!?! And you *still* look fantastic, even though you're 94!?!!

■ HERE they are – Glenda's Referendum Romeos!?!

● **Dominique de Villepin** – France's dishy new Prime Minister. When I say "Non" I mean "Oui"!?! Geddit?!?

● **Jan Peter Balkenende** – He's the dishy Dutchman from the land of tulips and windmills. When I say "Nee" I mean "Ja"! Geddit?!?

● **Jack Straw** – Britain's Foreign Affairs supremo!?! Sorry, Jack – in your case, when I say "No" I *mean* "No"!?!?!!

Byeeee!!!

THE INTEGRAL ROLE OF DEEP THROAT IN AMERICAN POLITICS

| 1974 | Deep Throat brings President Nixon to his knees as he's impeached |
| 1998 | Deep Throat brings President Clinton to his knees as he's almost impeached. |

"Blimey! He's good…"

ARCHBISHOP CRITICISES 'LETHAL MEDIA' FOR 'DISTORTION AND CYNICISM'

by Our Religious Affairs Staff **Lunchtime O'Pews**

A BEARDED half-wit yesterday ranted incomprehensibly about the media instead of focusing on his own problems i.e. that the only people who go to church are gay vicars and mad women bishops and anyway he doesn't even believe in God I read it in the *Sunday Telegraph* and he's only spouting all this rubbish in a desperate attempt to get publicity for his rotten church which no one goes to except gays and women bishops why should we take any notice of a man who doesn't know how to shave and wears a frock for a living? and yet he's got the

Paranoid loony: Dr Rowan Atkinson

nerve to accuse us of making things up well I heard it on good authority that Old Beardie has nicked all the lead from Canterbury Cathedral roof and *(cont'd Psalm 94)*

That Archbishop's Damning Indictment In Full

"The role of the media in contemporary Britain, whilst necessarily compromised by its enmeshment in the dictates of the commercial imperative, is nonetheless open to justifiable

criticism when one examines the layers of subjective motivation which lie behind the imagined independence of the editorial process, especially when filtered through the supposed demands of topicality which is itself conditioned by the paradigm of an auxiliary framework modelled on (cont. p. 94)

Sun WORLD EXCLUSIVE

Amazing revelations about the late Princess of Wales from the explosive new book *'Diana's Dead, So She Can't Deny It'* by her close friend and confidante Simoney Please.

Includes the following incredible scoops:

● *Princess Diana slept with President J.F. Kennedy and then shot him in Dallas in 1963 as revenge for his dumping her in favour of Marilyn Monroe.*

● *Princess Diana had a passionate fling with the sexy Indian-born Mahatma Gandhi. "It was lust at first sight," she said, "but he refused me because*

he was dead."

● *The Princess rated all her lovers with marks out of ten. Elvis Presley was 3/10, Prince Philip was 8/10, but the Loch Ness Monster topped the list with a sizzling 11/10. "He pressed all the right buttons," the Princess told Simoney shortly after her fatal accident.*

THE SUN SAYS

WHERE were you when you heard the news that Princess Diana had slept with J.F. Kennedy Junior?
Says Sun editor Rebekah Wad, *"I remember exactly what I was doing. I was giving this silly woman an enormous cheque for a load of bollocks".*

SIX TO WATCH

ONCE again the *Eye* puts you, the tennis fan, in the picture with our up-to-the-minute selection of the six top women tennis players in the modern game who will be competing for the coveted Wimbledon trophy.

Olga Legova,
(Russia), 21, blonde, long-legged beauty from the land of the potato.
Eye rating: Phwoarr!

Maria Scorchova,
(Ukraine),19, busty bombshell from the land of Lada.
Eye rating: Phwoarr!

Irina Lechova,
(Belarus),18, gorgeous pouting temptress from the land of the collective Tractor Factory (now World of Diesel).
Eye rating: Phwoarr!

Korka Fornikova,
(Russia), 17, blue-eyed nymphette from the land of Solzhenitsyn *(Surely 'beetroot and mosquitoes'? Ed.)*
Eye rating: Phwoarr!

Anna Gruntan-groanova,
(Chechnya), 16, flaxen-haired, tanned cutie from the land of ethnic terrorism *(Is this right? Ed.)*
Eye rating: Phwoarr!

Timella Henwoman,
(G.B.), 38, dark-haired English hopeful from the land of over-priced strawberries and warm champagne *(That's enough Six to Watch, Ed.)*

PINK TURDS TO RE-FORM FOR LIVE8

by Our Showbiz Staff PHIL STADIUM

THE GREATEST rock band in the history of the world, The Pink Turds, has announced that it is to re-form in order to save Africa.

The lead singer of the legendary 60s popular singing group, "Spiggy" Topes (now Sir Spigismond Topes, O.M., K.G.), has told a packed press conference yesterday, "The Turds have not performed live for 20 years, mostly due to the fact that the others are all dead."

He continued, "To be honest, we have not spoken to each other for decades but we have decided not to let such trivial matters stand in the way of our being given the top job at Live8 of abolishing poverty forever.

"When Bob rang me to ask if I was still alive, I could not say no to him.

"This will be a gig to remember, as it will be an extraordinary moment when today's audience can once again hear the unique sound of Topes, together with the late Raymond Fortescue-Watson, Justin Jervis Protheroe and Sydney "Sid" Weems, our legendary drummer."

Said poverty campaigner and event organiser Sir Bob Fockoff last night, "It is great news that the Turds are back to headline the greatest rock'n'roll show the world has ever seen."

Nelson Mandela is 106.

Old Nursery Rhymes

Byers!
Byers!
Pants
on Fires!

New-look GCSE Latin Primer

How to decline:

Asbo	I terrorise my neighbours
Asbas	You complain to a policeman
Asbat	He does nothing
Asbamus	We come round and set fire to your car
Asbatis	You (plural) move to another neighbourhood
Asbant	They say the situation is under control thanks to the new Anti-Social Behaviour Orders

---

IS IT TIME FOR A GAY TORY LEADER?

AT THE risk of sounding old-fashioned, we have to say that we still have misgivings about senior homosexuals declaring themselves to be Tories.

This is not mere prejudice, since nowadays there are many openly Tory individuals in all walks of life and being a member of a minority group like the Tories should not be held against anyone in public life.

Nevertheless, for many gays, the thought of what Tories get up to in private seems unnatural and unsavoury and their activities strike many as *(cont. p. 94)*

Andy Murray Greatest Tennis Player Ever

ANDY MURRAY's incredible achievement in winning Wimbledon (*He won two matches. Ed.*) at the tender age of 18 means he is unquestionably Britain's greatest tennis player ever (*He just won two matches. Ed.*), one who is now odds on to win every major tennis title this year, making him the youngest ever winner of the Grand Slam (*He only won two games. Ed.*), which means he is in fact the greatest tennis player of all time. (*You're fired. Ed.*)

Andy Murray To Earn Ten Million Pounds

EXPERTS say that should Britain's latest tennis sensation, Andy Murray, win every tennis tournament in the world next year, he'll earn TEN MILLION POUNDS!!!!

Tennis experts say the chances of Andy Murray winning every tennis tournament in the world are highly likely unless, of course, he gets beaten like he did at Wimbledon in the third round, but the fact he stands to earn TEN MILLION POUNDS next year proves he's the greatest of all tennis players and means we can continue to fill pages over the summer because we've got to fill up pages with pointless articles about him earning TEN MILLION POUNDS somehow (Cont. p. 94)

'WHY I BACK DAVID CAMERON TO BE TORY LEADER'

By Former Shadow Chancellor OLIVER LETWIN

● Because he went to Eton, like me.

© *The Sunday Torygraph*

"I think it's time it was put down"

APOLOGY

IN RECENT years, we may have inadvertently given the impression that those seeking refuge from tyrannical regimes abroad were being less than honest in their motives for entering this country.

Headline such as "Go home, you benefit scroungers!", "We must be asylum suckers!" and "Sod off, foreign scumbags" may have led readers to believe that we at the Daily Mail were less than sympathetic to the plight of these refugees.

In the light of the Zimbabwean crisis currently embarrassing the government, we now realise that these poor, unfortunate men and women are nothing less than heroic victims of misjustice, glorious rebels in the name of freedom and a jolly useful stick to beat Blair with (*Surely "noble champions of democracy"? Ed.*).

We apologise for any confusion caused to our readers and say 'hats off to the brave Zimbabwean martyrs – may they stay here for ever'!

© *The Daily Mail*

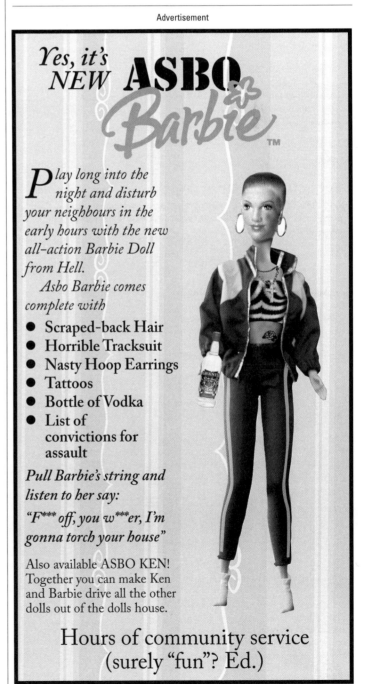

The Daily Telegraph At 150

Bill Deedes Remembers The First Edition

I WAS only a cub reporter at the time and I was sent to cover the siege of Sebastopol. What a challenge for a young chap freshly down from Harrow! The Crimea was a foreign country then, full of Russian chaps up to no good. Nothing much has changed from that point of view! The Russian Bear is still up to his old tricks and in 1855 I witnessed them at first hand. The thing I remember most vividly was eating caviar at the Headquarters of the expeditionary force and remarking to Lord Cardigan that *(cont. 1994)*

DAILY TELEGRAPH, FRIDAY, JUNE 29, 1855

The Telegraph

The launch of a new newspaper demands what may be known in the future as 'a mission statement'.

The Daily Telegraph is an impartial commentator on the public realm. It owes no allegiance to any party. We shall examine each issue on its merits, without fear or favour.

And we shall conclude in every case that the Tories are the rightful rulers of Britain and that a vote for them is a vote for a happy, prosperous and great nation at peace with itself and at war with everyone else.

The Royal Courts of Justice

Mr. Justice Cocklecarrot, at the Old Bailey, yesterday sentenced Sir Roy Meadow, the quack and mountebank, to death for a number of offences where wretched women have been wrongfully imprisoned as a result of the doctor's mendacious testimony.

IS THIS LORD LUCAN?
by Dominic Sackwell-Lawson

A MAN who bears an extraordinary resemblance to Lord Lucan has been spotted in charge of the Light Brigade. The fugitive Earl, wanted in England for the murder of his children's nurse, has sought refuge in the ranks of the British army.

"I would have known him anywhere," said one observer. With his bushy moustache and aristocratic bearing there can be no doubt that this is the scoop of the century *(You're fired. The Barclay Brothers)*

MATTHIAS

1st Elderly Gentleman: I must get my eyes tested.
2nd Elderly Gentlman: And why is that, sir?
1st Elderly Gentleman: Because it says here in this newspaper report from the Crimea that we are on the same side as the Frenchies.
2nd Elderly Gentleman: Gadzooks, sir. So it does...

TO THE EDITOR OF THE TELEGRAPH

POVERTY IN AFRICA

SIR – Dr Livingstone's ill-advised campaign to bring an end to the poverty of the African natives, well-intentioned though it may be, is doomed to failure. Indeed it may have the opposite effect.

Those of us who have spent any time in the dark continent know full well that the natives of that blighted land are incapable of managing their own affairs, corruption is rife and the leaders of the tribes have shown themselves to be greedy and cruel in equal measure.

Yet Dr Livingston, a saint in the eyes of a deluded minority of his admirers, persists in telling us that the savages, for let us not mince words here, are impoverished only at the hands of the European nations and not as a result of their own wickedness and folly.

Dr Geldof would do well to turn his attention away from Africa and to the suffering of his fellow Irishmen, so many of whom have perished through lack of sufficient potatoes, due to the callous indifference of the British Government *(Is this correct? asks the Editor)*.

Yours
Sir Willoughby Gusset,
Royal Tunbridge Wells.

Announcement

Mr Charles Dickens, the famous author, will be at W.H.Smith and Sons (Booksellers and Stationers) in Cheapside to sign copies of his new novel 'Oliver Letwin' (or 'A Man Forgotten')

School News
St Cakes

Empire Term begins on this day. There are 128 scholars in the House. The Rev. Ebenezer Aloysius Kipling (M.A., Oxon) has been appointed Headmaster, following the untimely demise of his brother, the Rev. Isiah Micawber Kipling (M.A., Cantab) who was consumed by cannibals whilst bringing the word of God to the natives of British Rumbabaland. H.R.T. Flashman (Bastards) is Chief Roaster of the Fags. Lord Snooty (Debretts) is Head of Pals. St Cakes Day will be celebrated on 12th July. The Speaker will be Lord Palmerston (O.C.) who will speak on "The Threat To Britain Of The Russian Bear". There will be a performance of Mandelsohn's Oratorio "Jeremiah" in the chapel performed by the School Orchestra with T. Brown, counter-tenor, attendance compulsory, conducted by the retiring Master of Music, Herr Herbert Von Toscanini. The Pugilistic Championships will be held on the Field of Blood (all scholars to compete) and will be judged by the School Chaplain, the Reverend Auberon St John Kipling. Leaves will be granted on August 29th. The new term, Prince Albert Term, will begin on September 1st. A fee of 16 shillings and 9 pence 3 farthings must be paid in advance by banker's order to the Bursar, Major (Retired) Algernon Kipling, 1st Buffs, C/o The Lodge, St Cakes, Solihull.

SPORTING INTELLIGENCE

The British gentlemen players at Wimbledon have failed to progress further than the first round, leaving the Continental players, once again, in undisputed pre-eminence on the lawns.

THE THEATRE ROYAL DRURY LANE
Grand opening of the new melodrama
'THE MOUSETRAP'
Limited season only

MISS ELIZA HURLEY, the popular Music Hall entertainer, delights her audience with a glimpse of finely-turned ankle.

ON THE OTHER PAGES

Filthy hospitals full of superbugs – says Florence Nightingale

◆

The new railways are far too crowded – says Sir Christian Wolmar

◆

Should the Lord Mayor of London impose surcharges on carriages entering the Metropolis?

◆

You decide. Write now to the Daily Telegraph with your verdict

---

PLUS
The fiendish new puzzlement that is sweeping the nation –
The CROSSWORD!

Exclusive in
The Daily Telegraph

I WAS THERE AS HISTORY IS MADE

by Our Man In Hyde Park **Lunchtime O'Booze**

NOT SINCE the creation of the world have we witnessed an event as historic as the global phenomenon that was Live8 – and the important thing is... I was there!

As millions of people all over the world gathered in Hyde Park to join their voices to the universal movement to make the planet a better place, I was right at the centre of history.

Alright, I had my doubts, but after five hours of non-stop drinking from some of the world's greatest bottles (Surely 'magnificent rock music' Ed.), brought together in the VIP area

for this incredible event, I too was moved to tears. Legendary names from the history of booze included Champagne, Gin and Tonic, Johnnie Walker, Kronenbourg 1664 and others too numerous to drink! Yes, it was a veritable galaxy of alcohol gathered together in one glass to unite all journalists of the world into writing this stuff. It was a night I will never remember. And the message came out loud and clear to the leaders of the world, "Where is the toilet?".

© All newspapers.

More of this 1 - 94

LIVE8 TRIUMPH

You've saved Africa, now how about my career?

Fock!

REB-8W
MAKE EUROPE HISTORY

Give us your fokking money!

GOD SAYS 'THANK YOU BOB'

by Our Heaven Staff
Angela Gabriel

YESTERDAY the Almighty saluted the most powerful man in the universe, Bob Geldof.

"I've been around for ever trying to do good and this bloke has just done it in a weekend. My message has always been 'the poor will always be with you' but Bob has proved me wrong – in a couple of days. I say hats off! If he

ever wants a job he can come up here and have mine!"

ON OTHER PAGES

- Mozart admits "Bono's the tops!" **1**
- Handel – "Madonna's still got it!" **2**
- Beethoven – "Thank God I'm deaf!" **94**

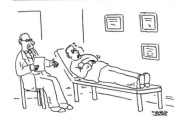

"That foul-mouthed voice that keeps telling you what to do...? I'm afraid that really is Bob Geldof"

GLENDA SLAGG

AN OPEN LETTER TO PIXIE AND PEACHES GELDOF

Dear Peachy and Pixies,

As a close personal friend of the family, I am deeply concerned at the way you young girls are turning out. I read that you're on the town every night in clubs and bars instead of staying at home and studying for your exams.

And I'm worried too by the company you are keeping – the photos of you with Z-list celebrities like Tara Rara-Boomdeeay send a cold shiver down my spine!

I love both of you dearly and deeply but you are in danger of turning from little English Roses into ghastly

slappers just like your mother – God rest her soul!

Your father Sir Bob is one of my best friends and won't mind me saying that as a parent he is a bloody disgrace who should be strung up whilst you two are taken into care for your own good!

You know how much your Auntie Glenda cares for you and you also know that if I didn't care so much I wouldn't write this open letter slagging you off publicly in exchange for a very large sum of money.

Yours, concerned,
GLENDA.

Daily Bush Telegraph

Africa, Monday

In the 21st Century, it is shocking to discover that in some countries in the world there are still children who are sent out to work wearing hardly any clothes and who are ruthlessly exploited by greedy employers. Take the case of Peaches Geldof in Britain

who though only 16 is required to write a weekly column for the ruthless Sunday Telegraph Group and to make programmes about teenagers for the greedy global media moguls at Sky TV. How long can we Africans tolerate this scandal that threatens to shame our (cont'd p94)

NO CONNECTION BETWEEN ISLAM AND TERROR

by Our Man At Scotland Yard **P.C. P.C.**

LONDON'S top policeman, Chief Superintendent "Knacker of the Yard" Knacker, yesterday called a special press conference in the wake of the London bombings to explain that in the view of London's police service there was no connection whatever between what he was about to say and common sense.

"Just because these bombs were let off by Muslims," he went on, "it does not follow that there is any link between the bombers and the religion of Islam."

"My officers," he concluded, "will be focusing their efforts largely on members of the Church of England and other fanatical groups – especially those who are known to be linked to extremist organisations such as the Women's Institute."

LATE NEWS
KNACKER'S TRIUMPH
Dead men arrested

INSPECTOR KNACKER last night announced that, "Thanks to a triumph of forensic detection" the four men responsible for the London bombings had all been arrested.

"The breakthrough came" he said, "when we uncovered evidence of the four men's identify, giving their names and addresses and the words "we did it – we want to be martyrs to the cause of Islamic terrorism".

RED KEN DEMANDS TWO-YEAR SILENCE

by Our London Staff **Pearl E. King**

THE MAYOR of London, Ken Livingstone, today called for all Londoners to observe a two-year silence about his disastrous meeting last year with the fanatical Muslim extremist Yusuf al-Kardawi.

"As a gesture of respect to myself," said the Mayor, "I would ask everyone to keep very quiet about the fact that I invited to London a man who preaches the kind of hatred that leads to people thinking that they can go round blowing up London."

"You can't say that!"

An Apology

IN COMMON with all other newspapers we may have given the impression that we deplored suggestions that there was some sort of link between the recent London bombings and Mr Blair's invasion of Iraq. Headlines such as "String Up Traitor Galloway!", "String Up Traitor Salmond!" and "String Up Traitor Kennedy!" may have led readers to believe that we felt it was in bad taste to make a connection between the two events, as these politicians had done.

In the light of the recent report by the highly prestigious and respected ISTBO (Institute Of Stating The Bleeding Obvious), we now realise that there may well be a link after all.

We apologise for any embarrassment to ourselves.

★ BAGHDAD TIMES ★
Friday 22 July 2005

LONDON 'EERILY CALM'

by Our Man In London

THE STREETS of London were eerily calm today as the city enjoyed its tenth consecutive day without a suicide bombing killing scores of innocent men, women and children.

It's hard for those living in Baghdad to imagine a place so tranquil and peaceful that it only has to endure one act of unspeakable carnage a fortnight (cont'd p. 94).

To all BBC news personnel

From Ms Helen Boaden-Catalogue, Head of the News Programme Programming Directorate

URGENT

The use in BBC news programmes of the word "terrorist" must cease forthwith. This emotive term suggests a value judgement which is likely to offend a significant proportion of our news-audience profile. In terms of our charter obligations it is vital in this respect to maintain a strict sense of neutrality. In future, those responsible for engaging in the delivery of explosive devices to users of the public transport system must on all occasions be referred to not as "terrorists" but as "members of the bombing community".

New link to open in time for the Olympics

●————————————————————●
KINGS CROSS   **BAGHDAD**

NB: Link also stops at Red Kennington

IS TONY BLAIR THE GREATEST MAN IN THE HISTORY OF THE WORLD?

DEFENCE EXPERT · SECURITY ANALYST · CONSPIRACY THEORIST

THE events of recent days have made one thing clear. Our prime minister now towers like a colossus over the world stage. Just consider the dazzling series of triumphs which have made him the greatest statesman of this or any other age.

First, he solved the problems of Europe. Then he solved the problems of Africa by abolishing poverty. Then he saved the world from the catastrophe of global warming. And that was just the start of it.

His next astonishing feat was single-handedly to bring the golden prize of the Olympics home to Britain.

But all this paled into insignificance beside the extraordinary fashion in which he rallied the nation's spirits in its darkest hour, following the London bombings.

Generations yet unborn will thrill to his Churchillian oratory which reawakened the British spirit of defiance: "I would like to thank the emergency services", "the police are doing an excellent job" and "we are looking at urgent new measures in relation to the prevention of terrorism".

There can be no talk now of Mr Blair retiring. Indeed it is unthinkable that he should ever be allowed to retire.

How would our world survive without him?

We would be left in a darkening world where terrorists would feel free to let off bombs in London streets, where millions of Africans were dying of poverty, where the icecaps would melt and where French farmers would continue to receive huge sums of money from the British taxpayer.

Absurd? You may think so. Yet it is this nightmare scenario which would engulf us all, were it not for the presence of Sir Winston Blair, the greatest man who ever lived.

© *Everybody.*

R A D I O   F O U R

What You Didn't Miss

THE TODAY PROGRAMME

Jim Naughtie *(for it is he):* ...and doesn't that mean that we're going to have to re-evaluate the whole way in which we attempt to structure our response to acts of... I'm sorry, we've run out of time for my question, so we'll have to leave it there before you can answer. And now, it's Thought For The Day with the Rev. J.C. Flannel.

Rev. Flannel: At this tragic time, when all our thoughts are going out to the families and loved ones of the bombers, there's been a lot of confusion and bewilderment about the role of Islam in all this. And I think it helps to remember what the word 'Islam' means. It comes from the Arabic word for 'peace'. And let's look at some of the other words used by our Muslim friends, which also give rise to a lot of misunderstanding. We often hear, for instance, the word 'jihad'. But how many people know that this means 'coffee morning'? So, let's not get distracted from the things that really matter in today's world. The most important moral challenge confronting us all today is the issue of whether women should become bishops. In a very real sense... *(cont. 94 kHz)*

PAKISTAN'S TOP-SELLING NEWSPAPER

DAILY MULLAH

22 July 2005

INSIDE THE SCHOOL OF DEATH

by Lunchtime No Booze

Our man goes inside St Cakes, the famous British Madrassa to see how students are brainwashed into the British way of life.

THE DAY begins with the sinister sound of a bell summoning the pupils to prayer. Here they listen to the fanatical ravings of the chaplain, Rev Tristan de Vere Kipling. His theme today "Keeping a straight bat in the great game of life".

Day after day they are subjected to a relentless programme of brainwashing which is designed to make them believe there are two sides to every argument and even more shockingly that one day England can win the Ashes.

I spoke to a typical pupil, Fotherington-Thomas (Barkworths) who unashamedly told me his mission in life was to "play up and play the game".

HUGE FEES

In his desk he openly showed me a copy of "his bible" The Wisden Cricket Almanac (containing technical details of how to make a century) and by his bed he had placed a photograph of the schools pin-up – Miss Liz Hurley.

Yes, on the outside Fotherington-Thomas seems like a typical easygoing teenager but inside there is no doubt that this confused adolescent has only one ambition, to end his life as a solicitor in Haywards Heath and *(You're fired, Ed)*

PARADISE

POETRY CORNER

In Memoriam Chief Superintendent 'Slipper of the Yard' Slipper, former head of the Flying Squad

So. Farewell then
Chief Superintendent
Slipper.

You were best known
For failing to catch
The Great Train Robber
Ronnie Biggs.

Now the Grim
Reaper has tracked
You down.
And you have been
Unable to give him
The slip.

E.J. Thribber (17½)

In Memoriam Tonino Delli Colli

So. Farewell
Then Tonino
Delli Colli.

You were the
Cameraman on
Such masterpieces
As *Once Upon
A Time In
The West,
Once Upon
A Time In
America*,
And, best of
All, *The Good,
The Bad And The
Ugly*.

All together
Now.

Da di da
Wah-wah-wah.

E.J. Thribb
(The Poet With No Name)

E.J. Thribb will be appearing at the Wye-on-Wye Literary Festival, reading from his new anthology *Wrong Sort Of Leaves On The Grass*. He will also discuss Sir Harold Pinter OM's new collection of war poetry *Fuck Bush* (Faber, £19.99).

CONSERVATIVE PARTY DIES

End of long and distinguished career

by our Political Staff **Simon Hefferhump**

AT THE age of 194 the Conservative Party lost its fight for life yesterday in a nursing home in Tunbridge Wells. The party was known to have been unwell for a long time, suffering a number of serious conditions including Hague's syndrome, IDS and, latterly, Howard's Disease, all of which left it weak and debilitated.

In latter years it became a tragic spectacle and did not even know who it was. Said one political observer Alan de Watneys, "It was a pathetic sight to see it in the House of Commons, unable to speak and getting grumpier and more bitter as the days passed."

O Heath, where is thy sting?

He continued, "This once great party was reduced to a shambling wreck."

Meanwhile tributes poured in from no-one at all as the nation failed to mourn the greatest political party in history.

William Deedes

The Tory Party I Remember

WHEN I first met Disraeli he struck me at once as an odd sort of cove. He wore green socks which is always the sign of a rum 'un. So when he passed the Reform Bill in 1867 I knew that we were in for a rough ride *(cont. p. 94)*

Damn!
I died before
Mrs Thatcher

That Heath Funeral Service In Full

Organ Voluntary
The Grocer Fugue
(Beethoven, arr. Heath)

Hymn
Morning Cloud Has Broken
(arr. Heath)

Reading
O Heath Where Is Thy Sting?
(Treaty of Romans, Ch.13)

Song
Three Days A Week
*(Lennon/McCartney,
arr. Heath)*

**The EUlogy will be delivered
by the Bishop of Brussels,
the Very Rev. Horace Sprout**

Anthem
I Was Sailing
(Stewart, arr. Heath)

Address
Arundells, The Close,
Salisbury.

Song
Signing In The Train
(Kelly, arr. Heath)

**Dismissal by Baroness
Thatcher**

*Order of service taken
from the Book of Common
Market Worship*

"Here we go then – another day, another Sudoku"

TEN THINGS YOU DIDN'T KNOW ABOUT HARRY POTTER

by Our Potter Mania Staff **Phil Pages**

1. 816,000,000 copies of the new novel are sold *every second*.

2. By lunchtime tomorrow everyone in the whole world will own at least two copies.

3. J.K. Rowling has made £94 billion this week – making her richer than the United States of America.

4. Dumbledore is an anagram of Leonardo da Vinci.

5. Harry Potter is a blood relative of Mary Magdalene through a long line of Merovingian wizards.

6. In the new novel a main character, Harry Potter, dies. He transmogrifies into Dr Who for the last instalment *Harry Potter and the Daleks*.

7. Ricky Gervais has been invited to write the next instalment of Harry Potter. J.K. Rowling is to appear in a new film of *The Office*.

8. Harry Potter's character was originally called Peregrine Worsthorne.

9. The K in J.K. Rowling stands for "Endeavour".

10. Over 8,000 billion stupid lists about Harry Potter have been published in the last five minutes. *(That's enough lists, Ed.)*

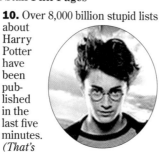

Pineapple-Chunks Gnome, age seven, gives us her exclusive view on the new Harry Potter

"I have not read the new Harry Potter book but my dad told me to make something up using the words 'magical', 'muggle', 'riveting' and 'complex narrative arc with deep moral undertones' – have I got that right, Dad?"

© Pineapple-Chunks Gnome 2005

"Cap'n Ahab won't like this"

BLAIR IN NEW CRONY ROW

by Our Political Staff **Simon Hogwarts**

THE PRIME MINISTER was embroiled in yet another scandal about "cronyism" when allegations about his friend Lord Voldemort surfaced yesterday in a document entitled *Harry Potter and the Half Million Pound Donation*.

One expert who has had access to the documents, Jemima, aged 7, said, "It is a complete mystery why Voldemort has been made a Lord. None of his contemporaries, such as Dumbledore or Snape, have been ennobled and to be honest, Lord Voldemort has a dodgy past involving the black arts."

She continued, "The only explanation that I can think of is that he has gone to Gringots Bank, taken out a vast number of gold galleons and given them all

to the Labour Party."

A spokesman for Lord Voldemort denied the allegations and said that anyone who repeated them would immediately be sued for libel and turned into a toad.

On Other Pages

● Australian Quidditch Team Thrash England In First Test – What Went Wrong? **1**
● Draco Malfoy gets ASBO **2**
● Your Trains Tonight **9¾**

POPE CONDEMNS HARRY POTTER FOR CORRUPTING CHILDREN

That's traditionally the job of the Catholic church

FATHER TO SUE LEADING PUBLIC SCHOOL

by Our Education Staff

A FURIOUS parent is to begin legal action today against St Cakes the famous Midlands independent school, after the headmaster, Mr R. J. Kipling, tried to expel his son.

The boy, who cannot be named for legal reasons, is called Fotherington-Barkworth (Silvesters) and has been accused of burning down the chapel and failing to get 12A*s at GCSE.

Said the headmaster, "I might be prepared to overlook the former offence as youthful high spirits, but the latter really does show that this boy is irredeemable".

Marlborough Country

Said the father of the alleged arsonist and exam failure, "It is grossly unfair that public schools and state schools have different standards on these issues. I pay a lot of money to St Cakes and in return my son should be allowed to do whatever he feels like".

"It's not as if that's all I do: I write poetry, I'm very much involved in charity work... why single out that one thing?"

What The Eye Says

THE SHAME OF BRITAIN'S BINGE LAW-MAKING

BRITAIN faces an epidemic of round-the-clock law-making which threatens to plunge the country into a new Dark Age.

Evidence is mounting to show that the government's policy of 24-hour law-making is producing nothing but confusion and chaos in the streets of all our major cities.

Citizens no longer have any idea of what is or is not legal, and many, it is clear, are so bemused that they no longer even know which country they are living in.

An only too typical scene of life in Britain today was witnessed by shocked observers recently in the heart of London's once-respectable Westminster, only a stone's throw from Buckingham Palace.

Groups of middle-aged men and women could be seen sprawling about on green, leather benches, in an all-night session of reckless law-making.

"I've never seen anything like it," said one horrified New Zealand tourist, Mary Maori, 26. "These people were totally out of control, just spewing out law after law. It was sickening."

We say this: *It is time this shameful madness was stamped out once and for all. There ought to be a law against it.*

"So much for us having the same attitude towards it as the Continentals"

DIANA ACCIDENT

'It was an accident'
SENSATIONAL CLAIM

Mary Ann Bighead

YES – IT'S THE big debate in the Bighead family. Should my daughters, Brainella and Intelligencia be allowed to watch television? There can only be one answer – NO. Because in the Bighead family we use our leisure time to do something a bit more intellectual than sitting around watching the goggle box!

I point out to Brainella that if she had wasted all those hours watching Celebrity Big Brother Island (or some such!) then she would never have completed her first symphony at the age of seven or written a novel at the age of nine. Meanwhile Intelligencia makes the point that living in a media-centric household they should perhaps be exposed to the wider culture of their peer group and their society.

This is a very clever remark coming from a three-year-old but I stand firm and suggest instead that we all play a fun family game such as translating the Odyssey from ancient Greek into Russian and back again. I can honestly say that in the blessed absence of the noxious cathode ray tube (!) the entire Bighead clan enjoyed a healthy balanced family evening together – except for me because I had to go off and be very clever on BBC TV's Question Time. Such is life!

© Mary Ann Bighead

The Alternative Rocky Horror Service Book

No. 94 A Service of Blessing for the Celibate Partnership of Same-Sex Ordinands

The President (*for it is he, or she*): Brethren and sistren. We are gathered here today to celebrate the coming together...

Congregation: Oooh er missus!

President: Titter ye not (*© the estate of the late Sir Francis Howerd*). As I was saying before I was so rudely interrupted, the coming together of M and M (*here he may say 'Rupert and Trevor', or it may be 'Jen and Fran'*) in the state of holy concelibacy.

(*The concelebrants will then step forward to the altar for the making of vows*)

President: Do you, M and M, solemnly promise to live together with your partner, M or M, for as long as you are both happy with this lifestyle arrangement?

Concelebrants: We do.

President: Do you solemnly promise to have but not hold each other, until such time as your relationship ceases to be meaningful in a real sense?

Concelebrants: We'll do our best, but none of us is perfect.

President: And do you solemnly pledge that you will refrain from all manner of hanky-panky, rumpy-pumpy and any other act of diverse lewdity whatsoever?

Concelebrants: That's a big ask!

President: I now pronounce you vicar and chaste partner.

(*Here the newly united will not exchange a kiss, as an outward and visible sign of their continence, one with another*)

READING
(adapted from Corinthians 13)

"Faith, hope and chastity, there abideth these three, but the greatest of these is chastity."

(*Here shall be sung a suitable piece of popular music, such as 'Tea For Two, Vicar' or 'Let's Not Spend The Night Together'. The congregation shall then recess to some suitable venue to toast the happy couple, as it may be with a cappuccino in Old Compton Street*)

Private Eye Rapped For 'White, Middle-Class' Bias

A NEW report has found that the satirical magazine Private Eye is guilty of an institutional prejudice in favour of directing its attacks on white, middle-class targets.

Says the Eye's Board of Governors, "There has been little effort to reflect the fact that Britain is now a multi-cultural society. Despite the changes that have taken place in Britain in recent years, the magazine continues to produce jokes about politicians, journalists and lawyers who are all predominantly male, white, middle-class and able-bodied."

The report cited as evidence an analysis of 25 'desert island' jokes carried by the magazine in the past five years. "In not one case," said the report, "was the castaway sitting under the palm tree depicted as disabled or of ethnic origin."

The report continued by pointing out that the "message in a bottle", traditional in this type of cartoon, was not once shown as being written in Gujarati, Urdu, Turkish, Albanian or Mandarin.

Said Lord Gnome, the magazine's proprietor, "We welcome this report and will be putting its recom–mendations into practice. In future my editors have been instructed to ensure that their satirical comment embraces the whole spectrum of today's vibrant, inclusive, multiplex Britain."

WHAT YOU WILL SEE NO. 1.

ਤੁਸੀ ਪਕੜਿਵ ਆਈ ਦੇ ਜਣੇ ਹਾਸ਼ਰ ਪੜੋ

POETRY CORNER

In memoriam Robert Moog, inventor of the famous Moog Synthesiser

So. Farewell
Then Robert Moog.
Pronounced to rhyme with
'Vogue',
Not 'fugue'.

Your invention
Revolutionised the
World of popular
Music.
Keith informs me
That it was used by
The Doors, Yes, and even
The Beatles.

Woeeeezzeeerrrreeeyyyeerdddooing!
It is hard to convey
The effect of your
Great invention in
A poem of
This kind.

>   E.J. Throob (pronounced to
>   rhyme with 'crib', not 'tube')

What was the Rees-Moog Synthesiser?

To anyone under 60, the name Rees-Moog might mean very little. But in its day the Rees-Moog was everywhere. Says one Rees-Moog enthusiast: "It was a truly revolutionary innovation, spewing out thousands of words every day over a vast area. It had a very distinctive sound: a kind of low, persistent drone that had the effect of sending people to sleep."

Said another fan: "The Rees-Moog could synthesise a whole week's news and turn it into a single unmistakable theme which could last for decades. One thinks, for instance, of The Return Of The Gold Standard, The Coming Second Ice Age, and Why The Tories Are Going To Win The Next Election Under Iain Duncan Smith."

To find out more about the Rees-Moog Synthesiser, log on to the Times's exciting new technology website, www.reesmoog.org.uk

---

"Er, let's see, I've got 'No to bullying', 'I love you', 'Say no to poverty', but I'm afraid there's no 'Jihad against the infidels'"

ME AND MY SPOON

THIS WEEK

No.94 SALMAN RUSHDIE

As one of the leading thinkers on the current state of Islam, and with your new book *Midnight Spoons* tipped to win this year's Booker prize, how do spoons fit into your view of the world?

My feeling is that traditional Islamic teaching on the subject of spoons is a symptom of the much wider crisis confronting the whole of the Muslim world, as it so signally fails to adapt to the changing context in which Islam is now having to operate.

But going back to spoons, do we find anything in the Koran which might throw light on the subject?

The failure of the Qu'ran even to mention spoons is irrelevant when compared to the irrational selectivity with which modern day Islamo-fascists have re-interpreted that book, oblivious to the fact that it is only essentially a historic document which is why when we try to…

May I just at this point…

…so the younger generation of Muslims experience a sense of alienation as they are brought up in a world so different from that which is…

At this point I usually ask whether anything amusing has ever happened to you, but I can tell that the answer is no.

NEXT WEEK: *Condoleeza Rice, 'Me And My Rice'.*

Help the Aged

In the twilight of their years Michael, Keith, Ronald and Charles have difficulty performing the simplest of tasks – staying at home, doing the garden, having a cup of tea.

Instead they are reduced to cavorting around the stage on a non-stop tour of the world. It is a sad sight but you have to remember that once these old gentlemen were lively free-spirited youngsters who enjoyed music and dancing.

But now in the winter of their lives their only pleasure is making money.

You can help Michael and his friends to live a normal dignified life by not going to their concerts and not buying any more of their albums

It's a small thing to ask but it would make a huge difference to the quality of their lives.

Please don't make any more donations.

Thank you

Help the Aged

"I'm afraid he's been radicalised by the Daily Mail"

IRA END WAR

It's no longer safe for our bombers to be on the streets

AIR TRAVEL MISERY

By Our Air Travel Correspondent
The Late Edward Heathrow

THERE WERE angry scenes at Heathrow yesterday when it was regretfully announced that a flight would not be cancelled due to industrial action.

Said one typical holiday-maker about to board the flight to Florida, "I am gutted. There is a test match on the TV, and I won't be able to watch it".

Said another disgruntled English traveller, "I only agreed to go away at this time in the sure knowledge that I would be back here in front of the telly by teatime".

Michael Vaughan is 94 not out.

OLD MEN GO ON TOUR – AGAIN

by our Entertainment Staff
Peter Tory

THEIR COMBINED ages may be 794 but there is still plenty of life in the ageing band of Tory leadership candidates better known to their millions of fans (Sid and Boris Johnson) as the "Polling Drones".

Crock 'n' Roll

Make no mistake about it, these septuagenarian troopers can still belt out the old hits of yesteryear as if there was no tomorrow.

And here they are again to play those immortal numbers that made you get up out of your chair and vote Labour.

"I can't get no satisfaction at the Ballot Box", "Time is not on our side", and "Let's spend less of the Gross National Product on wasteful bureaucracy together".

Malc Rifkind is strutting his stuff at 83 and Kenny "Hushpuppy" is still puffing on his trademark cigars at 87.

But no one cares about their age. In fact no one cares about them at all.

You can catch the Polling Drones at the following venues: *Daily Telegraph* p.9 • *Daily Mail* p.7 • *Saga Magazine* p.94, next to piece about holidays in Norway.

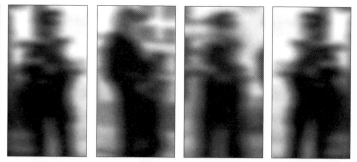

GOVERNMENT REINTRODUCES CAPITAL PUNISHMENT

by Our Political Staff **Lunchtime O'Noose**

IN A new crackdown on innocent men in the street, Home Secretary Charles Clarke last week ordered a return to capital punishment for anyone whom the police mistake for a terrorist.

"It is time these innocent people were taught a lesson," said Mr Clarke, who explained "capital punishment of course only applies to those shot in the capital, London".

Old jokes revisited

Why did you shoot him 8 times?

I ran out of bullets

WAR ON TERROR DAY 94

■ THE WHITE House has confirmed that it will no longer be referring to the ongoing conflict in Iraq as the 'war on terror', saying the term had too many negative connotations.

"From now on we'll be referring to it as 'Desperate Housewives'," said a White House spokesman, "as our market research has shown that this will make the ongoing instability in the country much less worrying to the American people".

"We're also considering changing George Bush to 'Bill Clinton' as that's also proving very popular."

HAVE YOU SEEN THESE MEN?

SPECIAL CCTV footage has been released today showing dangerous armed men who ran amok on the London underground killing innocent civilians and spreading terror throughout the capital.

Police were appealing to Londoners last night not to come forward and to say nothing at all in the hope that everyone will forget the whole thing.

"If you recognise any of these men", said a spokesman, "I would keep very quiet in case they shoot you."

HAVE YOU NOT SEEN THIS MAN?

HAS ANYONE in Britain not seen this man, known only as Sir Ian Blair, in the last 24 hours? He is rumoured to live permanently in a television studio somewhere in London but may occasionally make the odd journey to his office where he is thought to be the head of the Metropolitan Police.

According to intelligence sources he is a fanatical believer in himself and claims that "shoot-to-kill" is the only way for his followers to achieve their peaceful aims (cont. p.94)

Punch 'n' Jihadi show

Daily Mail

ENEMY IN OUR MIDST

by Our Award Winning Columnist **Phil Space**

ALL OF BRITAIN wakes up this morning knowing that we have a new and horrific enemy in our midst – a home-grown cancer that must be excised for any means possible.

I am speaking of course about the evil Cherie Blair, who perpetrated an atrocity of a speech when she defended terror suspects' civil liberties in Malaysia.

Revelations that Cherie has happily lived generously off the State in a home provided by the tax-payer for years makes her betrayal of Britain even more sickeningly repulsive.

And how does this woman repay Britain's generosity? By daring to suggest *(cont. p.94)*

(cont. p.94)

MAIL COMMENT

AS IF the current terror facing Britain wasn't bad enough, we now learn that two of last week's would-be suicide bombers were living on state benefits.

Wanting to blow us all to smithereens with their bombs is one thing.

But claiming state benefit is a far more serious matter.

Until such time as the police institute a policy of shoot to kill against all people known to be in possession of housing benefit forms, none of us can ever sleep soundly in our beds again.

RADIO FOUR

What You Switched Off

THE TODAY PROGRAMME

Radio 4 Announcer: And here is the news. The police are continuing their search for possible suspects in the terrorist bombing campaign.

Naughtie *(for it is he)*: As you've just heard, the police are continuing their search for possible suspects in the terrorist bombing campaign. Phil Airtime, you've got the latest on this police operation... what are you hearing?

Airtime: Well, Jim, the reports we're getting from the police suggest that they are continuing with their search for possible suspects, but obviously detailed information is scarce for security reasons.

Naughtie: So, what you're hearing from police sources is that detailed information is scarce. Is that for security reasons, Phil?

Airtime: That's right, Jim. Detailed information is scarce, but what we do know is that this operation is ongoing and we are assured that the search is continuing for possible suspects.

Naughtie: And do we know who these possible suspects are, Phil?

Airtime: The police are not saying a lot about it at this stage, but what I'm hearing from my own police sources is that they're not saying a lot about it at this stage.

Naughtie: Thank you, Jim. And at 7.58, the news headlines.

Newsreader *(B. Perkins)*: Police are continuing with the search for possible terrorist suspects. The BBC has learned that the identity of the suspects cannot be revealed for security reasons. Back now to James Naughtie.

Naughtie: It's 7.46 and time for Thought For The Day and the speaker today is the Imam Mohammed Rusbridger of the Frinton-on-Sea mosque.

Imam: You know, it's very easy, isn't it, to jump to conclusions, but you know the message of the Koran is that there's good and bad in all of us.

Naughtie: Thank you, Imam, and later in the programme we'll be bringing you the update on today's police operation as they *(cont. every day)*

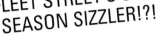

GLENDA SLAGG

FLEET STREET'S SILLY SEASON SIZZLER!?!

■ HATS OFF to Posh!?! At last someone's had the guts to admit that books are boring and we don't want to read 'em!?!? Let the snooty eggheads sneer but I say this – what's wrong with Posh just reading a few articles in glamour magazines and newspapers like this one!?!? We'd all rather read Auntie Glenda's words of wisdom than the latest Booker Snoozerama from someone you've never heard of!? You're alright in my book, Posh, even if you won't read it?!?!

■ *POSH SPICE!? What a disgrace!?! What sort of example are you setting to your kiddies when you say you haven't even read Harry Potter?!? Talk about illiterate!?! We always knew you were stoopid but we didn't know your kids should be taken into care as well?!?! We should throw the book at you, Posh, not that you'd read it!?! (You've done this, Ed).*

■ PAULA RADCLIFFE!??!?! Arenchasickofher?!? OK so the skinny beanpole has finally won something – Hoo-Bloody-Ray!?! It's about time too you big quitter!!? And this time you even did it without peeing in public – pardon my French!? Who cares?!? You're not even worth writing about!?!?

■ *PAULA RADCLIFFE!?!!! Donchaluvher!?! Britain's marathon miracle with the* fastest legs on earth!?! When all the other athletes were a droppin' and a floppin' on the track only plucky Paula put some pride back into Britain?!? And without pooping herself to boot!!?! – Excuse my French!!? Three cheers for Golden Gal Paula!!?! Hip!Hip!Hoo Cares!!?! (Is this right?? Ed).

■ SO BRIDGET Jones' Diary is back in the Independent!?! Do you know what this single gal thinks? V. bad idea!!?! Geddit?!!.

■ SO JUDE and Siena, Kate and Crackhead Pete and Sadie and some other bloke are all back together or split up, I'm not sure which!?! Give us a break Mr Noozman and write about something else?!!.

■ HERE they are – Glenda's Bank Holiday Bonkers:

● Omar Bakri – OK so he's a bearded nutter!?! But he can inflame my passions anytime!!?

● Sir Ian Blair – London's new supercop?!? If you can't find Terror's Mr Big you can always find <u>my</u> phone number in the book!??! Be seeing ya, Big Boy!!?!

● Shane Warne – Here's one maiden you can bowl over any time you like Cobber!?!? Geddit!!?!

Leg-Byeeee!!! (Geddit?!?!)

DISTRICT HOSPITAL ALL DEPTS →

WARNING HOSPITALS CAN SERIOUSLY DAMAGE YOUR HEALTH

Maily Telegraph

FRIDAY, AUGUST 19, 2005

MARILYN'S LOVE SECRETS REVEALED – WAS SHE MURDERED BY JFK?

PLUS More pics of gorgeous girls in this year's hot bikinis

PLUS SUPER SEXY SUDOKU p. 28

OI, BEARDIE, BUGGER OFF!

THE MAD MULLAH of Neasden, Lurpak Bashir-al-Luni, last night continued to pour out a litany of hate from the pulpit of his North-West London mosque in Neasden's leafy Tesco Street (now renamed Jihad Crescent).

Al-Luni told 20,000 screaming followers (Sayed and Dorissa Bonkir), "Rise and destroy the infidel wherever you find him".

And, if this was not enough, the Mailograph has learned, this crazed imam now wants the British taxpayers to buy him a new hearing aid on the NHS (estimated cost £39.70).

THE TELEGRAPH SAYS ...

Enough is enough. Wake up, Mr Blair, and send this potty Paki packing!

The Latest Stream Of Poison From Neasden's Hate Cleric

● "The West is in a state of total corruption and decadence"

● "We should rise up and kill Queen Victoria. She has a lot to answer for"

★ BAGHDAD TIMES ★

Friday 19 August 2005

HATE FIGURE FLEES BRITAIN

by Our British Correspondent Omar Bakri

MUSLIMS worldwide were celebrating last night as news spread that the preacher of hate against Muslims, Tony Blair, had fled Britain for a sun-drenched villa in the Caribbean.

"Blair's departure is a day of great celebration for all Muslims," said one leading Islamic Cleric speaking from Lebanon.

"Blair's preaching in support of George Bush's illegal invasion of Iraq and the subsequent slaughtering of countless thousands of innocent Muslims is an abhorrence to all right-thinking people."

Muslim leaders said they hoped that other extremists who backed the war would now follow Blair's lead and flee the country to ease tensions in Britain.

LEGOVER MAN SEIZES THRONE

by **Casin O'Booze**

THE 25 inhabitants of tiny Monaco were rocked to their foundations yesterday by the news that the throne of their miniature 800-year-old Principality had been hijacked by a middle-aged sex fiend.

He is the 47-year-old Prince Albert of Legovia, best known for his thousands of love-children.

Monaco Grand Pricks

Said the unrepentant new monarch, "I have only done this to boost the population of my new kingdom to the point where we can have a referendum on the EU constitution."

How He Is Descended

Grimaldi the Clown	Old Mother Kelly
The Brothers Grimmaldi	Ned Kelly
Jo Grimondi (former British Liberal leader)	Gene Kelly
Garibaldi	Henry Kelly
Countess Rainier Spencer	Kitty Kelly
Claudio Rainieri	W.G. Grace Kelly
Wayne Roonieri	Amazing Grace Kelly

Prince Rainier = **Grace Kelly**

Prince Albert of Legovia

"This is nice – sun, sand, sea and sudoku"

That New Democratic Iraqi Constitution In Full

1. Everyone shall be entitled to have a share in the governance of Iraq except the following: Sunnis, the Baath Party, non-believers, women, anyone except Shia clerics.

2. The greatest natural resource of Iraq is oil. This to be shared equally between a) the Kurds; b) the Shiites; c) the Americans.

3. Er...

4. ...that's it.

Signed G.W. Bush *and whichever Iraqi ministers have managed to survive 'friendly fire' by US occupying forces this week.*

NEW DEMOCRATIC IRAQI CONSTITUTION

It's one man one vote...

...and I vote we get the hell out of there

BLAIR BACKS BLAIR

by Our Police Staff **Lunchtime O'Penfire**

THE Prime Minister took time out from his busy holiday yesterday to give his unqualified public support to the man at the centre of controversy over the London bombings.

"Blair has done an excellent job," said the Prime Minister, "and he has my complete confidence. There is no reason for him to resign and it would be ludicrous for a man with all his experience to leave his job just because of one tiny mistake in invading Iraq."

The Prime Minister concluded: "Blair is the only man fit for the job, and I see no reason for him to step down and hand over to Gordon Brown.

"Now, if you will excuse me, I have got to go and put on some weight."

Sir Ian Blair is not on holiday.

Happy Retirement From The IRA

POLLY FILLER

THANK GOD! The long summer holiday is almost at an end. Like most working mums, I've been at my wits' end counting the days until it's all over and I no longer have to take Charlie swimming, cycling, paintballing, Science Museuming (again – yawn!!), visiting his little friends or trailing round Blockbuster looking for the latest Playstation kids game (*Pimp City: The Brothel Wars* since you ask!).

And, as you may have guessed, I've had zero help from the useless you-know-who (Simon!), who has spent the whole holiday in front of the television watching *Pro-Celebrity Sewer Diving* with Jeremy Clarkson and A.A. Gill.

It's been hell and I don't know how I've coped – but now it's only 17 hours and 47 minutes until the summer holiday is over – the **nanny's** summer holiday, that is! And I tell you one thing – I'm never giving her three days off again. The sooner Rebeccah gets back from Gaza ("family crisis" supposedly!) and gets on with reading Charlie the new Harry Potter book and washing Simon's underpants – or is it the other way round? Men! They're all the same – the better for all concerned. I tell you, these last few days have been so exhausting that I need a holiday – so I'm off to Dubai until term starts, for some serious sun, sea and shopping. Salaam!

© *Polly Filler*

'A' LEVEL RESULTS
Are Standards Falling?

"I got an A,S, B & O"

Ken Pyne

ONCE again this summer's 'A' Level results have been published in the national press and record numbers of fruity girls have been seen celebrating on the front pages.

Yet the worrying question remains. Is it becoming easier to get into the Daily Telegraph and the Times?

Phwoar 'A's At 'A' Level!

Statistics claim that an astonishing 97% of girls taking 'A' Levels this year have now appeared in national newspapers, prompting fears that standards are slipping. Said one educational expert, "Last year we were told that the girls were the fruitiest ever. Now this year we are meant to believe they are even fruitier. I'm sorry, I just don't believe it."

Wa-Hey Levels!

Newspaper editors were, however, quick to defend their performance. "How dare you question the fruitiness of our 'A' Level girls? They are every bit as fruity as last year, if not more so. They fully deserve their results, ie appearing on the front pages of all national newspapers."

Not On Other Pages
■ Boys getting their results

Official UCAS clearing list

September 2005

Places are still available on the following courses

BA Hoodie studies Three part modular study involving field research and dissertation into contemporary Hoodie issues.
Bluewater University, Kent
The Lakeside College, Essex
Brent Cross Institute, London

BSC Ipodology Four year programming course including commercial downloading, party shuffle and troubleshooting options (special subject: unfreezing after you've only had it a month).
The University of e-bay, online
The Google Polytechnic, Llandudno
Computers R Us University, Guildford

BA Binge Drinking Management 24 hour course involving Bacardi Breezers, vodka shots, Kronenberg 1664 and Strongbow cider.
Hope & Anchor College, Moss Side
Wetherspoon University, Leeds
The Coach & Horses, Soho

(That's enough courses, Ed).

DAILY MAIL

IS IT FALSE OR NOT?

BEFORE | **AFTER**

by Our Hair to the Throne Correspondent **Maddy Tup**

THE question everyone in the office (me, Barbara, Courtney and the girl from work experience, who I think is called Stephanie but I may be wrong) was asking last night is: is our story about Prince Charles' hair weave completely false?

The signs are all there. The story is so thin. It has no roots. It's just a bald lie. But yet the strands have been woven together in such a way as to fool people into thinking it was the genuine article.

What do you think: Is this story genuine or fake?

Call the Daily Mail wig line, and ask to speak to Barbara, Courtney or possibly Stephanie, because I'm going on holiday as soon as I've finished this hair piece *(geddit?)*.

EDEXCEL

GCSE Religious Studies
Paper One

1. Do you know anything about Religious Studies?

a) Yes b) No c) Don't know

2. If your answer to question one was a), b) or c), would you be available to mark some exam papers for us?

a) Yes b) No c) Don't know

3. The money is quite good and it'll only take you twenty minutes or so, go on please, I'll buy you lunch, would you get back to me asap?

(Time allowed to reply: 3 weeks)

What You Missed All Week

THE TODAY PROGRAMME

The Nation's Favourite Colour

Humphrys: And now it's time for the poll that has set the whole nation talking – what is Britain's favourite colour? From your thousands of nominations, our experts have produced a shortlist of just five colours. Today we're looking at the first of the five – the colour blue.

And here to make the case for 'blue' is Steve Sarnie, the Gombrich Professor of Visual and Media Studies at the University of Stoke Newington.

Sarnie: It is understandable why so many of you have gone for 'blue' as the colour which gives you the biggest buzz. I mean, just check it out. The sky is blue. The sea is blue. So, obviously, the big money is on blue. Stands to reason, doesn't it??

Humphrys: Thank you, Professor. Well, I certainly like blue. I mean, I may not know much about colour, but I know what I like. Ha ha ha ha. What about you, Sara? From that face you're pulling, I suspect you're not a blue person?

Sara Montague *(for it is Carolyn Quinn)*: Well, we're doing 'yellow' tomorrow and, to be quite honest, if it was a choice between 'blue' and 'yellow', it's got to be 'yellow' for me. But it's not what I think, it's what the listeners think that matters.

Humphrys: Since when?

Montague: So, it's not too late for you to take part in our great 'Favourite Colour' poll. You can text or email your choice of colour to philairtime.bbc.co.uk and the result will be announced on this programme on September 25th.

Humphrys: And tomorrow the case for 'yellow' will be put by the nation's favourite Rabbi, Rabbi Blue.

(Preview tape of Rabbi Blue)

Blue: Hullo, Sara. Hullo, John. I was visiting a dear old lady in hospital the other day, and she said, "Lionel, the trouble with this place is that they don't serve custard". And, you know, that set me off thinking about the colour yellow. Especially since my friend had jaundice.

Montague: So there's something for us all to look forward to tomorrow. Is it time for some news yet?

Humphrys: No, it's time to tell you what's coming up later today, here on Radio 4.

(Silly music)

Serious Voice: We take it for granted. But we couldn't do without it, and it changed the way we live for ever. Michael Portillo traces the history of the coathanger. Don't miss him. Radio 4, 11.30am.

(More silly music)

Another Serious Voice: 'Afternoon Theatre' at 2.30pm presents The Coathanger, a new play for radio by W.W. Wentworth. The harsh life of an Edinburgh heroin addict is changed forever when he discovers a coathanger in his wardrobe.

(More silly music)

Silly Voice: And a welcome return at 6.30 this evening for the ever-popular Coathanger Quiz, with team captains Stephen Fry and Sandy Toksvig. Their guests tonight, joining in the coathanger fun, will be Michael Portillo, Ann Widdecombe and the Glaswegian playwright, W.W. Wentworth. Don't miss it!

(Listeners switch over to Radio 3 and then quickly to Classic FM)

So our death was a tragic accident

Just like this sculpture

ON OTHER PAGES "Was sculptor drunk?" – Eye witness shock account p.94

CLARKE ADMITS 'I WAS WRONG'

by Our Political Staff **Peter O'Bore**

THE veteran Conservative leadership contender Kenneth Clarke last night admitted that he had been wrong in supporting the Tory Party.

Speaking from his home in the Nottinghamshire village of Hushpuppington, Clarke frankly admitted, "When it was launched, I thought the Tory Party was a great idea and would work".

EU Turn

"But I now realise that it was always doomed to failure. This is why I am now putting my name forward to lead the party to its fourth successive election defeat."

Kenneth Clarke is 165.

Now out on DVD

Fu Mandy-Chu And The Evil Trouser Mountain

(Rating: EU)

MILLIONS of Chinese trousers are advancing on Europe. Only one man stands between them and the end of the French textile industry.

The moustachioed Spin Doctor Fu Mandy-Chu sets out singlehandedly to stop the evil tide of wily oriental trousers taking over the world, with his legendary catch-phrase "Me not quitter, me honourable fighter."

Alas, he fails.

HIRE SIX SAMURAI AND GET ONE ABSOLUTELY FREE!

A YEAR IN PICTURES – 2

BUSH ON THE BIG ISSUES

BUSH MEETS McCARTNEY FAMILY

BUSH SIGNS TRADE AGREEMENT

BUSH MEETS INDIAN LEADER

BUSH GETS TOUGH